HEAT THE FURNACE
SEVEN TIMES MORE

PATRICK McGEOWN

Heat the furnace seven times more

introduction by

Professor Asa Briggs

READERS UNION
HUTCHINSON OF LONDON
1968

Originally published by Hutchinson & Co (Publishers) Ltd. Reprinted
for Readers Union by Hollen Street Press Ltd, Slough.

Contents

Contents

to Aileen my wife

Introduction

by Asa Briggs

Professor of History, the University of Sussex

I T is easy to make generalisations about society, not least
about attitudes to work and play. The generalisations are
often clothed in rhetoric, often in jargon. Sometimes they take
the form of exhortations, exhortations to *other* people. Any
direct personal statement, honest enough to convince, read-
able enough to capture attention, dealing fully not with the
general but with the particular, is sufficiently rare to command consideration. Indeed, where such statements have
come down to us from the past, like *The Wheelwright's Shop*,
they have acquired a special status as documents in social
history.

Mr McGeown's book seems to me to be this kind of docu-
ment. Steel has been his life, but it has not been the whole of
his life. He describes simply but vividly what it has meant to
work in the steel industry during the twentieth century.
As a boy he was 'steelworks bound': there were no options. In
maturity, in 1945, the 'big thought' in his mind was 'what
would happen to our trade'. The conditions of ownership
did not diminish his sense of involvement. 'The firm provided
the wherewithal, but I made the steel and therein lay my
self-respect and my prestige.'

In describing both the events of his life and his attitudes to
work and life he is imaginative without being sentimental,
and he can convey the sense of noise and heat and effort to

readers who have never shared his experience. His chapter on 'the art in manual labouring', the art of bearing 'the daily burden of tiredness and boredom equably, to know the limits of one's strength and to husband it' touches on themes which are not usually expressed in words. He always describes his work and the work of his workmates with pride. He fancied himself with a fourteen-pound hammer. He noted as a boy the satisfaction of the first-hand melter 'as he watched the metal stream from his furnace into the waiting ladle'.

Only in maturity did he realise the full implications of changing technology—less wear and tear on the human body and mind; less individual art, more precision. Not the least interesting aspect of Mr McGeown's picture is the place of technology within it—another subject about which it is very easy to generalise from outside. He came to feel like an 'anachronism' as techniques changed and as new men came in—which are the more disturbing?—but he never lacked perspective. In his recollections he avoids all nostalgia and treats retirement from the industry as 'a chance to put a little even tenor in my life'.

We have clearly moved a long way from the chronological landmarks which stand out not only in his experience but in the experience of millions of people in this country—the First World War; the general strike; the years of unemployment; the Second World War; the Labour government of 1945. It is revealing to study Mr McGeown's personal reflections on what is now one of the most familiar of all historical sequences. In discussing the general strike, for example, he comments succinctly on the difference between the viewpoint of the miners and the steelworkers ('ours wasn't a hating trade'); in a chapter on the years of short time and unemployment, he quietly explains that if he had a reason at all for gratitude to the depression 'it was for missing so many months of nightshifts'; when he comes to the Second World War he is 'intrigued' to wear a uniform (of the Home Guard) for the first time in his life at forty-odd years of age. His book is a kind of general assessment of personal experience, an attempt to fit everything into place on paper as it has been fitted together in life, and just because we have already moved so far from *his* landmarks what he has to say becomes of very special interest.

Even his topographical landmarks—and he has a keen sense of place—are beginning to be distant from us. He enables us to understand why people have been attached to places that travellers would never have bothered to visit, not least because he can feel his way behind industrialisation to what had been there before. 'I liked Craigneuk, I thought it was a grand place and I liked the name of it too. I was sure there was history in it but I never found out. I was sure too that it had been a beautiful place before the advent of slag tips and belching stacks.'

For all Mr McGeown's ability to express common experience, he could not have written this book unless there was something very distinctive about himself. In his last chapter he talks about the writer in him, of his idea of heaven being 'a small cheque', of his sitting for 'O' level in English Language and in Literature, of his interest in the W.E.A. and in adult education. He came to believe that in every steelworks there should be a library, where books on technology would not be the only books. Clearly he set out throughout his life to extend as well as to deepen his experience. He also looked for the kind of independence that can so easily be taken for granted, but which a minority of working men have slaved to acquire ever since the industrial revolution. His book is the book of a man who has found independence: it should be treasured as such.

The Word is Goodbye

It was all over at last, forty-eight years of it. I saw my relief mate walking up the melting shop and I lifted my haversack and raincoat from the furnace cabin, and went to meet him.

It was nine o'clock on a snowy Saturday evening in February, and the long line of steel furnaces were almost deserted. On each one only a first-hand melter, the leading hand, remained; the junior hands had all sloped off a few moments before their time. The firm expected every furnace complement of four men to stay at their posts until their reliefs came on. It often happened that way, but on a Saturday evening men were restless, they felt they were missing something extra in the clubs and pubs outside.

I met my mate down by the D. furnace, 'She's all yours, man,' I said; it was the steel furnaceman's time-honoured way of saying that all was well. He humped his haversack a little higher on his shoulder, grinned tiredly, and answered, 'O.K. Paddy,' and made to move on. 'Just a minute Dick,' I said, pushing out my hand, 'It's more than good night, it's goodbye.'

This time he really did shake off the appalling nightshift tiredness, to wish me the best of good luck. 'I had forgotten you were finished tonight,' he apologised, 'I forget nearly everything on this blasted shift.' I believed him, that was the way night work affected me too. Especially when one was getting on, and Dick, like myself, was an oldtimer; another two years and he'd be shaking them all farewell too.

It would be a sorry day for him when it happened, for he

loved steelmaking, and despite his habitual weariness he had no wish to quit. His father had been a steel furnaceman in Middlesbrough, and his grandfather had puddled wrought iron somewhere in the West of Scotland. 'It makes me a natural,' he always said, 'I've got liquid steel for blood, and a steel billet instead of a heart.'

I met quite a lot of the father and son tradition in the steel trade. My own father had been a steel furnaceman for the greater part of his working life, first in Scotland, and then England. The tradition wasn't always a matter of sheer love and devotion to the trade. It was a matter of expediency, either make steel or starve.

The melting shop had a warm and cheery look as I walked along. It always had on cold winter nights, and although home was inviting as always, I didn't relish stepping into the snow. I stopped at the B. furnace to bid good-bye to the four melting shop cats. They lay drowsily happy on a piece of sacking, and were little concerned about my retirement. Yet I was their best friend, the one man who fed them regularly, for with most steelworks' cats it is often a feast or a famine. I hoped the famine would never be too prolonged in their case.

Before I reached the end of the shop the nightshift men started to stream in, and it was handshakes all the way. It was nice of them but I hate being a central figure. It had me muttering gibberish in my embarrassment. When it was over I went down the steps at the end of the A. furnace, and clocked my time card for the last time.

Now that the nightshift men had gathered in, there wasn't a soul to be seen. The works was always quieter each evening when the day men quit at five, and the Saturdays after one o'clock were the quietest times of all. Only the whistle sound of a diesel locomotive on the blast furnaces reminded me that I was standing in the heart of a modern steelworks. The quietness persisted in my long walk to the main gates.

Once outside them I stood to look back on the place where I had earned my living from when I was a boy of seventeen.

It had given me bread, and I had given it plenty, the sweat of my brow, my strength, my health, my youth. Was it worth it? I had time to think it over. One thing, I had gone out under my own power, and another, I had no bitterness. That hasn't always happened in my trade.

Facing Retirement

Retiring at sixty-five didn't break my heart. I was tired and glad to get away. Four years previously I had suffered from pneumonia, and after that it never was the same. I found it a burden getting to work and an even greater burden getting home from it. In between wasn't too bad. The works lay a mile from my home, across the other side of the Ship Canal, and I could see it if I turned the corner where I lived. Nevertheless there was a big difference between my locality and the steelwork town. The one was residential, somewhat, and the other was working class, plenty.

I was working class plenty too; I was not ultra proud of it, not ashamed of it. It was there whether I liked it or not, and if sometimes there had been avenues of escape then I must have missed them. As soon as I retired my income had ambitions that way too; it shrunk from a weekly pay packet of around twenty-five pounds to one of between eight and nine pounds. The total included a combined pension of £5. 12s. 6d. for my wife and me from the National Pensions Board. There was also £3. 7s. 4d. monthly from the Iron & Steel Confederation, and a monthly pension of £7. 3s. 0d. from my former employers. This, plus the fact that I own my home plus a few pound notes yearly from investments, made me confident enough about the future.

Added to this was weekly board from my wife's unmarried sister Josie, and a Government weekly grant for our mentally retarded daughter who is also named Josie. My daughter was twenty-six years old when I quit work, she has always remained at home with us, and is a completely innocent and happy fragment of humanity. Her mentality is that of a child of eight, and I could be exaggerating at that. She is a neatly built frail little girl with only the merest command of language. She doesn't stammer, but once outside her meagre vocabulary she has great difficulty in pronouncing her words. Even today I find it hard to understand her. There are often bad moments for both of us, she in her agony of endeavour, and I in an agony of misapprehension. She is completely unaware of the hard world outside, and of mortality. To her, her parents and her aunt will never grow old. If it were only true for her sake! But we all three are old.

We would like to see her die before us, it would create great sadness within us but it would banish the even greater sadness of wondering what will become of her. It could happen that way, for I cannot see long life for one so fragile. Yet she is seldom ill, she loves life, and her sense of fun is pronounced.

Her sister Bernadette is twenty months younger. She is a fine looking girl who hurts neither my eyes nor my heart. Her husband John Pennington is a scriptwriter for radio and television, and she manages their book and record shop a mile from my home. They are both of an age, and they are bang in the times they live in. I'm glad they are, for it's a terrific world to be young in. It's shaky and chancy and chockful of wonders, and it's grand that I've some one who knows how to use it.

The steelworks pension pleased me very much, though compared to many occupations it was no money at all. Indeed that's just what it was a year or two previously, no money at all. That's what made me happy, to be around when they were dishing it out, and me still able to count it. It was a voluntary award from the management to long-serving employees, and with my record I reached the top figure. Every month I hand it to my wife and she lays it aside for our light, coal, and gas bills. She also keeps all of our national pensions to help run the home, and I rub along on the three pounds odd per month which my trade union pays me.

As well as being useful, my works pension helps my spirit a lot. It makes me feel as good as the next man, for I would have been a sad and bitter fellow indeed to have gone out with nothing at all after a lifetime of skilled and strenuous labour. I know some old men who are fixed that way. I sympathise with them and I avoid them, for they have only the one sad subject, and it is very boring. Old! Poor! Bitter! It is too bad.

We were discussing working men's finances one night in one of the furnace cabins. It was interesting talk, simple talk, for that sort of finance is usually simple. A man draws his weekly packet and pays his way, if there's anything left over it goes for the thing he longs for most. It may be a yearly holiday, a deposit on a house, a car, whatever it may be it is usually achieved if health and employment remains steady. But the dream rarely comes true if there is a weakness for gambling or drinking or mismanagement in some other way. We decided that any workman who possessed one thousand pounds and owned his own home was sitting pretty. I'm not very pretty sitting or standing but I qualified, just. But I kept the knowledge to myself, it was my business and since it had taken me forty-eight working years to acquire it, there didn't seem much to boast about.

Whether I boast about it or not, I'm darned happy it's there. I fight tooth and nail to see that it remains there, just a few ciphers tucked up in a book. The pound can deteriorate, dehydrate, or disintegrate, I don't care, even if its worth decreases, my thousand pound is still doing its job. It helps me sleep at night, and it saves me from being a man of straw. I had to climb a few mountains and breast a few rivers for that thousand. I had to go through the jungles of betting shops, bingo halls, fruit machines, and pubs. They were all there waiting for me, rubbing their hands as I opened my pay packet, knowing my weaknesses. How the deuce I acquired my fortune I just don't know.

When I quit the steelworks it was 1963 and for most of the years between 1945 and then we had been busy. There had been only one recession in trade that I remember. But it had percussions and its own little tragedies. Ours was the number one melting shop, the less modern of two. During our busiest years we were an eight-sets shop, that meant we had eight regular groups of men to man the furnaces. If there were eight furnaces in commission then the regulars were employed on their own furnaces. If one furnace, or even two furnaces, went down for repairs, a general maintenance job of three or four weeks, the furnacemen were still busy. They stepped on to the one, or two spare furnaces which were lit up to replace the others. If more than two furnaces went down for maintenance the men were still all right. They shared the work available and probably welcomed the odd laying off day.

Then came the recession in trade in 1958 and a change in policy on the management's part, and the shop decreased from eight furnaces in commission at peak time. It became a six-furnace peak time shop. By agreement between management and the trade union branch, the eight sets of melters reverted back to six sets. That meant that only the senior men in each grade remained static, the juniors stepped back one grade, and that's where the tragedy came in. The junior first-hand melters went back to being second-hand melters, the junior second-hands became third-hands, and the junior third-hands became furnace labourers again.

It didn't disturb me because I was a senior man, very much so, and in the British steel trade seniority is strictly adhered to. It disturbed me to see good workmen, more than that, they were skilled men, having to let go the greatest ambition they could think of, and that was to be first-hands. To be men in charge of steel furnaces.

The junior third-hands, young vigorous men, wouldn't have made steelmaking their trade if that goal had not been there. They were married men with all the commitments of modern man, so they had to stay to less wages and less prospects. The junior second-hands were worse off, they were all in early middle age, and a step back meant their chances of becoming first-hand melters had vanished. They'd be old men before their time, ending their working lifetimes in steelmaking's hardest job of all, which is always the lot of the second man on steel furnaces. The regret of the junior first-hands was the keenest of all. They had climbed the mountain, and the air was good, and they liked the view, and now they had slipped and they lacked the stamina to get back again. They were men of fifty years and over, and to do a second-hand melter's job again was beyond them. It needed lungs of brass and the stamina of a bullock to open tapholes and release the surging metal. They tried and they hung on, and they lay off exhausted, and they came back again, but the life and the heart had gone out of them.

Unlike other trades steelmaking is very much a stationary affair, a man's fortunes usually begin and end on the one melting shop. He can quit if he likes in the middle of his career, or at the height of it, and start in another melting shop, but he'll start at the very bottom again. The reason for this is the system of promotion by seniority, and the thread of promotion is a thing jealously guarded by every man on a steel furnace. He knows to the day who is senior to him and who is junior, and if Vulcan himself came on a melting shop he would start at the bottom.

Steel melting too is different from most other skilled jobs, for the melters do not serve apprenticeships to the trade in the usual way. One reason is that at no point of the trade was it ever a youth's occupation, from first to last steelmaking needed a man's strength. Even in these progressive days a steel furnace is no place for immature youth. There are plenty of young furnacemen, just a year or two in the trade, who could operate huge furnaces if given the chance. There are also plenty of senior men operating huge furnaces for years, who wouldn't be really skilled melters if they lived and worked for another hundred years. They get by, just, with the aid of the system, but the bright young melters don't grumble. They come into the melting shop with their eyes open, they weigh it up and if they like it they stay, if they don't they go. Most of them realise that the seniority system, while not faultless, is the only one to ensure fair play. John Hodge, one of the pioneers of our present Iron & Steel Trades Confederation, knew that when he, and others, laboured for a system that made the bosses' favourites take their turn with the rest.

When I quit I was happy to know that a reverted man would take my place, and that he would take over a job worth having. I had been a first-hand melter for twenty-two years, ever since I was forty-three years old. Previous to that I had worked as a second-melter for twenty years. This was a tremendously long stretch without promotion to leading hand, but it coincided with the great trade depression between the two world wars.

Most of the time I had no feeling of urgency about it, for there was much to be learned about the second man's place on a steel furnace. There was plenty to worry about too, if one was the worrying sort, and I was just that. Indeed a quick promotion from there to that of a leading hand would have just about set me crazy altogether.

However, towards the end of that long period of exhausting labour I was very anxious to step the one rung higher to the prestigious position of first-hand melter. When men on steel furnaces turn forty years old and have not reached the top, it is a time for long, long thoughts.

I hated to do it, especially since steelmaking is a friendly trade, but I used to look at the leading hands who were sixty-five and over, and wonder when they would give some one else a chance. I resolved too that if I did become a leading hand, and lasted as long as they did, I'd make for the gate and stay out.

Many a man in many a trade and profession promised himself the same way, and failed to fulfil it when the time came. I didn't forget, but my inducements were enough to make it no act of heroism. The men who retarded my progress in the years prior to the second world war had no superannuation to look forward to. In their situation I would have acted just as they did.

It may have been shame on the firm's part, but since there was no superannuation then, there was no set age for retiring. I believe in a set age for retiring and where there is none I'm suspicious. I don't think it is due to consideration for the older men, rather do I think it due to indifference to both old and young. On steel furnaces, which is the only trade I'm acquainted with, the young are more important than the old. They should get their chance and one unfailing way to insure it is early retirement, and superannuation to make it worth while.

If someone in authority had come up to me and said, 'You are fifty-five, and we are grateful that you gave us your best. So take this horn of not so plenty, but enough, and go rest beneath the old apple tree,' I'd have gone gladly, for at that age, with a decent superannuation, I could call it retirement, or if I liked I could call it a change of job. There would be still time to enjoy it either way.

In spite of the exhausting conditions steelmaking had a very attractive side. To the first-hand melter there was great satisfaction as he watched the metal stream from his furnace into the waiting ladle. He had an awareness of creation; seven or eight hours previously this surging white-hot liquid had been one hundred tons of solid limestone, steel scrap, and hot iron. He had controlled the huge flame which played over the metal, saw that it did its work, and that it didn't damage the furnace's brick roof or linings. Hour after hour he had tended it, watched for every change in the liquid, increased the slag contents with more lime, or thinned it out with iron ore. His junior melters were every bit as interested as he was. It was their money too that was filling the ladle, and their sweat too that put it there.

Sometimes the satisfaction went awry. The liquid didn't gallop out of the furnace generously but trickled out in a miserable taplike stream. That wouldn't suit any one, and least of all the foreman who was responsible for tapping the charge successfully. The melters would rush hurriedly to the front of the furnace, and clear the obstruction away with long iron rods. The liquid, if it was in good condition, would spurt away again, the melters would wipe their streaming brows, and the foreman would resume his former attitude of omnipotence.

The foremen's traditional title was Samplepasser. It stemmed from the days when technology in the steel trade was more elementary. When the state of the metal and its readiness for tapping from the furnaces was judged by the grain of broken metal samples. A melter would dip a long spoon through the furnace door, and pass it swiftly through the bubbling slag to the metal beneath. It would be cooled off and hammered for the samplepasser to inspect.

Nowadays the samplepasser, or superintendent, as modernity has it, still is the authority, but he looks to the laboratory to confirm his practical knowledge. I'm not certain if all samplepassers are practical men on the most advanced steel plants in Britain. Technology is more and more decimating personal skills, but where I worked they were all former first-hand melters of vast experience.

Their experience was no greater than mine at the latter end of my career, but I wasn't foreman material, I recognised that early in my working lifetime. The management recognised it too for they never asked me. They did appoint one or two who were ill-fitted temperamentally for the job, that was no one's fault for the choice was very limited.

Through the years the samplepassers I knew were mainly sane well-balanced men. Having experienced every form of furnace hardship themselves, they made things as light as possible for the melters. I left that type behind me when I moved out, Artie McGowan, Big Andy Blane, Tommy Wright, Harry Thornton, Jim Watson, Bob Young, Charlie Barnaby, O. Baily, legendary men in steelmaking. The firm doesn't really know how lucky they are to have them.

There's lots of things the higher ups never knew about the men I worked with. It was impossible that they should know of the devotion and care and pride that went into steelmaking. I often pondered over it and wondered how such excellent qualities might receive justifiable recognition, but there was nothing I or any one could do. The immediate management, the melting shop managers, respected them always but even they never sensed the depths of it. Those melters in their love of their work went far in excess of what the firm paid them to do. They were perfectionists and a damn nuisance to the rest of us who were otherwise. They were of a class, small but always present, that has existed since ever metal was wrought in furnaces. They should not have been in commercial melting shops, where men toiled only for money from firms that existed only to make it. Like the armourers of legend the steel they wrought should have fashioned Excaliburs.

I admired them but I was not one of them, and when possible I kept away from them for they never knew when to rest. In steelmaking I steered a middle course, I wasn't the best and I wasn't the worst, but at times, especially on the nightshift, I thrilled at the sight of it all. There was drama in the bright-lit noisy melting shop, and the sweating men. It was there too when I looked across at the rolling mills and saw the bright ingots, fresh from the soaking pits, crunch in the rolls of the cogging mill. I'd tell myself that I had helped to make those ingots and I would watch the strip grow longer and longer, from bright heat to dull red, and I would listen for the swish of the saw as it cut through them like butter.

But an hour or so afterwards, when the sweat was pouring from me, and I was lashing manganese into a streaming ladle at 28 lb. a shovelful, then it was different. With my sweat towel covering my face to the eyes, to save me from scorching, and the dust of the manganese building a solid wall in my lungs, I saw little drama in steelmaking at all. I'd be asking myself what had gone wrong in my living that I should be there, while out in the world the bright clean clever men were asleep.

It was as bad in the winter when the alarm clock would sound at half-four in the morning, and I'd fight with the sleep until nearly five before rising. I always got along with little sleep on the early turn, it was the only week in three when our evenings were free. Usually I went to bed after midnight and read awhile, for reading in bed was compulsive with me, then fell over asleep about 1 a.m. It wasn't enough but I knew it would do, for so long as I could stand on my feet I'd pull through.

It was always a relief to get into the bright warm melting shop from out the cold dark mornings. If the luck was with me and things were easy, I'd have a sleep for an hour at the back of my furnace. It was a foolish thing to do, for the black gas fumes and the dust had their own way with me then. I'd waken up feeling like a man sick of a palsy, but I knew that it was the old palsy of the night before that was the root of it. I always swore to myself that the next night would be different, that I'd be abed at 9 p.m. like the wise ones among the melters. But it rarely happened, for there were so many things to do when a man was young, and had only free evenings every third week. There was no sense in it, and if there had been sense in me there would have been no life in it. I would just have been eating and sleeping and waking and making steel. And that was a bad way to live, I could see the result of it all around me in the grim cheerless souls who humped on and off the steelworks. Still, there was less sense in mixing steelmaking with too much living. I could see the results of that too, in fact I followed some of the results on their way to the cemetery. Good men they were too, makers of bright lights even if their own did go out prematurely.

The lifesaver for me when I was young was the afternoon turn, from two o'clock till quarter past nine. Officially the relieving time was ten o'clock, but the earlier hour meant a leisurely drink in the clubs and pubs before going home. I made it my storehouse of sleep; it made up for all I had missed the previous week, it kept me going for all I would miss on nightshifts the following week, for I never had the happy faculty of sound sleep in the daytime. Even as a boy in a Scottish steelworks, where I worked twelve-hour night and dayshifts in alternate weeks, I still found real sleep uncertain. The one day I'd be restless and jumpy for want of it and the next day I'd be a dead man for eleven hours.

Sometimes my mother in her pity would let me miss work and sleep on, and the following evening she would waken me at five to be ready for six. Then not all the household could convince me that I had missed out for a day and a half.

That was in Craigneuk, where I was born in 1897.

3

Where I was born

There was nothing lovely about Craigneuk. It was, and is, about twelve miles from Glasgow, and a centre of heavy industry.

Steelworks, ironworks, coalmines, are not beautiful but they have their moments. I liked Craigneuk, I thought it was a grand place and I liked the name of it too. I was sure there was history in it but I never found out. I was sure too that it had been a beautiful place before the advent of slag tips and belching stacks. Even my uncritical eyes could see that.

That was before the Irish and the Poles and the Lithuanians arrived. Most of them penniless and none of them welcomed by the Scots. Only the most broadminded of heavenly beings could have welcomed that lot. I don't know about the Poles and the Lithuanians but the Irish had been coming from the end of the eighteenth century. The first Roman Catholic church was opened in Paisley in 1808, and the first Roman Catholic school was opened in Glasgow in 1817. They were built by the pennies of the Irish immigrants. There were 120,000 Irish born residents in Scotland in 1841, and they were still packing them in, in overcrowded ships from Londonderry and Belfast. The ships *Londonderry* and *Thistle*, both less than 300 tons, often carried 1,700 people at a time. Even in good weather the journey would be uncomfortable. It was very cheap, sometimes as low as sixpence per head, and there was no Avilion at the end of the journey. Most of them landed up in the disease-ridden Glasgow slums, where 60 per cent of the population lived in one-roomed homes, and where in 1832 more than 10,000 people died of Asiatic Cholera.

No wonder the Scots didn't think much of the Irish, or their Roman Catholic religion. It was no consolation that many immigrants were not Catholics, but Orangemen. It only added to bloodshed and distress when the rival factions met on St. Patrick's Day and on the 12th July, the celebration of the Battle of the Boyne.

Still they were there, and the Scots had to learn to live with them. They had even to tolerate a lot of inter-marrying. For it wasn't unnatural for a Scots Jeannie to fall in love with an Irish Paddy, even if her Paw and Maw referred to him as, 'That Irish Pig.'

Ah well! The Scots are no' sae bad. No sae bad ata! I liked them fine and I was an Irish Paddy too, and a Catholic to boot. To boot? That rings a bell! By jings it does, as we used to say in Craigneuk long ago.

The Irish came chiefly from Mayo and Galway, the hungry counties in the west. And from Derry and Donegal in the North, and they were hungry too. My parents came from Co. Armagh, and according to them it was the hungriest one of them all. They were born in neighbouring townlands, my father in Granemore and my mother in Athnagurk. My father's people farmed a piece of stony land on the side of the Brague mountain, and in between the men travelled to the Scottish harvests. The women stayed at home to look after the cow, if they were rich enough to have one, and to feed the hens.

My mother's people on the other hand were almost urban, they flocked in to the linen mills in Darkley village. A few hundred people lived there in tuberculosis-ridden tenements, set in the heart of a beautiful countryside. My mother was a millgirl there and she earned a daily sixpence for twelve hours work.

When the millowner died they started to build a monument to his memory in the town two miles away. It was never finished, and it wasn't pulled down. Years later I saw the unfinished heap myself. No one could tell me what it represented at all, but they all called it the Monument. According to my mother, the builders, the pair of them, stopped work one day, scratched their heads and said, 'Why the hell should this fellow get a monument to his memory. What's he done?' They went up and down the town fruitlessly seeking an answer, and wouldn't go back without one.

My mother loved that town; actually it had only three streets, short ones, but to her it was the great metropolis. It had a market hall and a clock above it, but the clock had never ticked in my mother's time. The town council, when they got round to it, had it repaired. It took them forty years, and all the English national newspapers solemnly reported the fact.

It was possibly the sixpence a day business, and other similar affairs that filled my mother with two great ambitions. The first was to provide a meal for her family, and the second was to know where the next one was coming from. I never knew her to fail in the first but she had some hell of a time galloping after the second. She was a great woman for broth, good rich broth. She used to say, 'In troth broth's a lifesaver.' I rarely answered her, for it isn't good manners to speak with a big spoon in my mouth.

Regard for her homeland remained with her to the end of her days and I doubt if she would have left it but for my father. He never had any intention to remain there, and she had no other intention but to be where he was. He was fond of Ireland too, but where she lingered over its beauty he spoke of personalities, of the boys who like himself had waited for the strength of men so to be up and away to the fascinating world outside.

There was little or nothing in Ireland for him, but if he had been fairly prosperous he would have gone just the same. It was a sign of virility, of awareness, of adventurous spirit, that a young fellow should be away from Granemore by the time he was twenty-one, after that only the cabbages remained. Some, especially those who went to America, never came back, but many did return to tell their experiences and to stir the blood of those who waited to go. They told of no ease or fortune but of hard physical effort, that was often dangerous too. But there were pay packets for doing it, and that was enough.

He had known my mother from when they were both very young, and they married in Ireland during one of his periods home from Scotland. They were of an age, twenty-five at the time and I'm sure he hankered for a home of his own after years spent in model lodging houses, farm bothies and cramped tenements. The one they rented in Cowie's Square could not have been smaller, and their first child died in it before I was born.

There were five of us in our one-roomed home in Cowie's Square. The earliest memory I have was of four years old, that would be in 1901. My brother Peter who is still alive, and still a steel melter, was two years old, and my sister Anna Mary was a baby in my mother's arms. My common sight was seeing my mother breast feed her. It was a very common affair with all the mothers in the square outside as well as in the homes. The mothers all carried their babies in big shawls, and one had to look closely to note that the baby was at suck. Very, very cosy they looked indeed in their mother's arms, and safe from the big world outside them. There have been perambulators in Craigneuk, but I never could remember any. Every mother seemed to carry her baby that way, and the shawl was an indication of the family's worth. The lovely soft grey ones of Shetland wool bespoke of the very cream of Craigneuk society.

Five of us in one room was a bit cramped, but the builders had spaced it out cunningly enough. The two beds were the hole in the wall kind, and curtained off from the room proper. The sink, with cold tap only of course, was under the only window. We had a wooden chest in which my mother stored blankets, and which made an extra seat, two chairs, and a table, and some shelves along the wall. That was the lot, and it was enough. If we had owned the classiest furniture in all Scotland we would still have lacked space. When the two chairs and the chest were in use the rest of us sat on the fender in front of the fire.

The terraced buildings in Cowie's Square were not all one-roomed homes like ours, 'Single-Ends' was the Craigneuk term for them. Just one flight above lived the aristocratic two-roomed families. They reached their homes by flights of stone steps at the back of the buildings. We single-enders reached our doors in the close that ran from the main street to the back. In each close there were four families living, and their pride of home and caste were indicated by bright brass plates which announced their names. To have a nameless door was to have a shameless life. There were quite a few nameless ones, for we were tough in the square. It had the toughest reputation in Craigneuk. A fact that made my father proud, though being a mild man he did nothing to uphold it. He liked as big a drink as any other Square male, but the more he drank the milder he became. To be a real initiate would have meant him joining the gang in their pavement club at the street corner. This my mother resolutely forbade. She had no fear of Harry the Bear, as the gangleader was known, or any of his aides, just a great distaste.

To reach the main road and avoid passing them meant her taking the most circuitous routes. This occurred often, for the corner was rarely unoccupied; on summer nights the gang slept there. Yet I passed them a thousand times without them raising their eyes from their pitch and toss, or their card school. Prideful people didn't like turning off the main road into the square. They feared observers would brand them as residents. Tradesmen too refused to turn their horse vans into it. Too many times they had lost sacks of coal, fruit and vegetables, and bakers' loaves. What the Square residents re-quired, they had to travel for, and with the money in their fists.

The Friday and Saturday evenings were always riotous in the 'Neuk' (all proud residents used the affectionate diminu-tive) and especially in the Square. The miners made revelry on their Friday paydays and the steelworkers on their Saturday paydays. My mother used to lock the door to shut out the sounds, while outside my brother Peter and me, and all the kids thrilled at the sight of the big policemen (mostly Highlanders) carting off the disturbers of the peace. Sometimes we aided the police by fetching the drunk's barrow from the station. This was a flat affair on which the violent were spreadeagled and tied, and trundled off to the cells. It was a most degrading sight, especially when a woman occupied the barrow. I watched in fascinated horror as she lay there dishevelled, sodden, beaten by life, and shrieking obscenities.

I should have been in bed, and so should my brother Peter, but there were no strict child-rearing rules in our home.

Sometimes, as if we weren't crowded enough, my mother would take in a lodger. Her idea was not for profit, not with the sort we had, but to tide them over a rough period. They were always Irishmen, newly landed, and seeking work. If they managed to find it they paid their way and moved out. If they were unlucky, then so were we, for they hung on eating what there was and paid nothing. Sometimes in desperation my mother had to gather up something pawnable to get them their fare back to Ireland.

At times like these my brother Peter and me especially were often hungry. We'd be like hawks watching the lodgers at mealtimes. If they moved or turned their backs for a moment we swooped on their plates. It was desperately disappointing each time the lodger learned to hold fast to his plate.

Every time a boarder entered Peter and me had to sleep on the floor. It didn't disturb us much, in fact I seemed to sleep better that way. Every night on shutting my eyes I pursued my unfailing ambition to keep awake until I finished my night prayers. I never managed once. However, I frequently achieved another ambition, to go to sleep with jujubes in my mouth and find them still there the following morning.

My parents got on very well together, although they didn't express affection outwardly. They hadn't the training, vocabulary, or desire to do so. I never heard them quarrel or raise their voices in anger, and I could hardly have missed it in our one-room home. They displayed no effusive affection to my brother and sister and me. There was no kissing, no hugging, no wrestling in fun, and we didn't miss it; their huge fount of goodwill towards us was enough. We took that for granted as our natural right, which it was. We took their serenity in each others presence for granted too, when really it was a great piece of good fortune for us.

We grew up without the least hint or training about sex. Nor did we ever mention it to each other, for we inherited the vast reticence of our parents. The result for me at least was a groping of my way through adolescence that almost tortured and bewildered me out of my mind. I think my brother and sister escaped more lightly, for they were always more stolid and stronger nerved than me.

Often I looked at life not as a great adventure, but with fear as my chief emotion. I suspect my mother, more than my father, was the same way in her youth. Most likely she found peace in her religion, but not for many years. Rather she found strength to battle her way to peace. We both had to shed the great burden of thinking that sex is a sinful thing.

Many of the Irish peasantry have the same problem, though it has lessened these last thirty years. It is the chief reason for so many bachelors and spinsters in rural Ireland. Poverty, I believe, is only a secondary reason.

I met many men of this type as I grew up among the Irish in Craigneuk, and I've met them in England too. They were all quiet men, manual workers on building sites, on road-making, and steelmaking, and leading the lives of great personal purity. They found consolation in the clubs and pubs, and in the end their drinking became lonely as they outgrew their generation. Usually they lived in small boarding houses, or homes run by Irish landladies. Often at the end these ladies buried them, and many a time I have contributed towards such a funeral.

There were other Irishwomen in Cowie's Square who

worked off their inhibitions in a way different to my mother. They rolled up their sleeves and went at each other with scrubbing brushes, and hair-pulling. Almost certainly the row would be over the use of the communal wash-house. Bored magistrates in Wishaw Police Court, a mile away, had been doling out fines for generations for breaches of the peace of this kind. The wash-house days and hours for each household were by rota, but very often aggressive ladies jumped their turn.

When the rightful occupant came along with her bundle of washing, and her sticks for the boiler fire, she'd be met by a scowling virago thirsting for battle. With arms akimbo, and her scrubbing brush at the ready, the invader would stand with a 'God save Ireland look' on her puss. In no time at all they would be at each other. Also in no time at all my illusion about Irish women took a bashing. With my mother's prompting I would keep thinking of them as gentle saints, even if they weren't all scholars.

Although the fifty or more households in Cowie's Square were 90 per cent Irish very few of them returned to Ireland. That didn't mean that they forgot their land and their race, nor that they were enamoured with the Scottish nationality and wished to submerge into it. They hadn't and they didn't, and the Scots didn't want them anyway, they preferred them to keep their distance. The real reason of course was lack of money, for a visit to one's hometown was expensive. According to the people back home every one who went to Scotland became a millionaire and was expected to act like one. Besides it only needed a shutting of eyes to the grim surroundings and the ears, three times out of four, transported one back home.

The place was grim indeed. It started from Borland's Land, a dreadful collection of tenement houses all blackened by the smoke and dust of the steelworks immediately adjacent. Once past there the steelworks main gate and offices came in view. If it was nearing five o'clock in the afternoon the wall would be lined with steel furnacemen who would soon start their nightshift. It would be their last few moments of relaxation before commencing their fourteen-hour shift. Most of them were tall, strong men who had been born away from Craigneuk, from the Highlands of Scotland, from many parts of Ireland, and a very few from Poland and Lithuania.

Each one would be dressed for action, for there were no lockers or baths or changing rooms then, and all of them would wear heavy nailed boots, which, in keeping with the tradition of the district, would be brightly polished. Employers had been known to engage men chiefly by the state of their boots. In fact Mr McFarlane, the steelworkers' manager would stretch every point to find work for any men who approached him wearing white sweat towels, and brightly polished heavy boots. They were worth looking at and they knew it, they were the aristocrats of the heavy industry world. Their wages stood out against other trades like skyscrapers in a town of two-storey buildings. The fact didn't make them more prosperous, for the rigours of their work on hand-charging furnaces increased their normal thirsts. Naturally many of them satisfied their thirsts often and long. But they were not degenerates, the harshness of their daily lives rarely seeped into their souls. They were very fine human beings, and I admired them hugely when I was very young. I was very proud too to see my father, Peter McGeown, standing with them, straight and strong, and as decent as the best of them.

Once past the steelworks offices, a railway bridge stretched across the main road. There's nothing so damnable as a railway bridge for spoiling the appearance of a road. On this one, night and day, there chugged eternally locomotives, crashing wagons and mingled with the warning screeches of steam whistles. I grew up with those noises, and the beat, beat, beat, of the works' powerhouses.

Once past the bridge there was Dymock's Buildings and opposite them was Stewart's Buildings, ugly tenements both, cheerless boxes. They lay at the foot of a brae where half-way up stood the steel melter's favourite pub, the Beehive. I was later to work as barman there. Farther on was my own Cowie's Square, and more tenements, pubs and shops. Interspersed on either side were rows of dreadful, blackened, one storied, one-room dwellings. Cowie's Square, and the other tenement's, had at least cold water taps and gas lighting, but the rows had communal street pumps and were oil or candle lit. When I was a child of two years in 1899, a plague of some sort swept through one long row, and left at least one death in every home. My mother grieved over that and often told me of Harry Gold. He had died too in his middle twenties, 'A fine man', she said, 'with curly hair the same colour as his name.' Harry played the big drum in the Irishmen's flute band; he cut a fine figure as they swung down the main street on their way to some gala day.

My mother loved band music and singing. She used to sit at the window knitting and waiting for the young miner's choirs to stroll past on Sunday evenings. They came from Hamilton town, three miles away, and from Wishaw town, a mile above the 'Neuk'. They took their singing seriously and always the old Scots songs. The people respected them and made way for them as they moved easily along. My mother loved it, she savoured every moment from the first sound coming stronger and clearer, to the last one fading in the distance. I liked them myself. It was one of the things somehow that lit within me a spark of lasting respect for the Scots in Craigneuk, and for Scotland. The sparks were lit many a time and remained lit. I liked the Scottish people, the working class, the only kind I knew. They were hemmed in by poverty, harsh labour, ugly surroundings, but always some culture and natural dignity kept seeping through the muck of their lives.

The tenements and the dingy rows on the main street were palaces compared to the dwellings surrounding the 'Craig' coal pit. It lay out on its own, half a mile away, an isolated miner's hamlet. The one-storey rows of blackened stone, bathless, waterless, oil-lit, were a depressing sight. There was no changing place at the pit, no drying place, and it was the wives' daily job to stand with knives in hand and scrape the muck from their husbands' working clothes. In their leisure time the miners were fond of whippet racing, and many in the 'Craig' owned these swift little animals. The dogs were their faithful companions too, and I used to see them sitting in the circles of conversing miners. The men were always hunkering down in traditional collier style, with the weight of their bodies on the one bent leg.

Not all of them lived in the cluster around the pithead. I used to see them walking down the Craigneuk main road on their way home, unchanged, unwashed, and the little naked pit lamps fastened to their caps.

Men returning to and fro from ironworks, steelworks, and mines, was the 'Neuk's' commonest sight. The miners always had their flasks of cold tea and their packets of gowdy cheese sandwiches. The steelworkers nearly all carried metal lunch-boxes under their arms and enamelled, deep-lidded tea cans in their hands. The ironworks depended more on their relatives carrying in their meals. It was a small iron works, just off the main road and it was appropriately named 'Mount Etna.' I used to carry in a neighbour's meals and watch him at work before leaving. His name was Maule and his job was puddling iron into wrought iron.

It was the most exhausting job of all in heavy industry. I was very young at the time and didn't realise the energy Mr Maule was expending. He stood in front of the small furnace and worked a heap of doughy, half molten pig iron into a roughly shaped ball. For this he used long iron rods and then the metal was taken out with long tongs and hammered. That was in 1907 when I was ten years old. Since those days I've never heard of puddling furnaces, or puddled iron, or puddlers. The old method would be uneconomical today, and I doubt if it was ever really improved upon. If there is a puddler today working on an old type furnace, then I'd love to meet him. I'd be gazing on a mighty man.

I think it is still possible to meet some oldtime melters of the cold-metal, hand-charging days. My father was a first-hand melter of that type in 1914, and they were still that type in Craigneuk by the end of the first world war. After that the machine-charging melting shop took over. It was a most important step forward, for steel was made quicker, and in furnaces of greater capacity.

However, long before Craigneuk experienced improved steel production, I had a most important step forward to undergo myself. I had to start school.

4

School

I was five years old in 1902 when I entered St Patrick's Roman Catholic Elementary School. It was a very old one-storied building and must have been built early in the nineteenth century. Beside it was the fine new church of St Patrick with room for many hundreds of parishioners.

I had little desire that first day to start my scholastic career, and neither had many of my fellow newcomers. We were in a babble of tears and all being soothed by anxious mothers. The little middle-aged teacher soon altered that; she was expert in her profession and had broken in many of the mothers. By the end of the day I liked the place and rather regretted that my education was completed. My mistake was rectified the next morning when my mother trundled me off for another go at it. After that I was no trouble, and Mary Kelly, a young girl from next door took charge of me and two other Cowie Square entrants.

A couple of years afterwards the old school closed and we moved into a fine two-storied building. We also for the first time had a male teacher on the staff. His name was Moreiety and he travelled twelve daily miles from Glasgow. It must have dented his salary for Catholic school teachers, especially, were very poorly paid at that time.

The headmistress, Miss Muldoon, would have welcomed Mr Moreiety ten times more if he had been twice his size. Actually she sought a protector as much as she did a new colleague, for St Pat's was very rough indeed. So rough that the saint himself must often have been tempted to come down from heaven, and have another go at converting the Irish.

27

As it was Mr Mo, as he soon became known, was small, light, and not at all aggressive. So Miss Muldoon had often to defend Mr Mo as well when the rough Irish Parents came barging in threatening murder.

She was a tall strong built spinster between forty-five and fifty years old, and could handle herself pretty well, but getting a bit old for battling.

Mr Mo put up with his troubles and stayed where he was teaching the sixth form. He was very good at it too, and a very likeable fellow. All the time I was there he remained the only male teacher, it still wasn't enough. One day the parish priest, Canon Ritchie, expelled a boy before the assembled school. I forget the offence but the boy, a tall ragged lad, stood before us and wild with venom and fear. The priest demanded he apologise to his form mistress. She was a beautiful girl and I wondered how any one could wish to offend her. For any time she bid me good morning I was set up for the day. The other boy had different ideas, he must have hated her for his words of muttered apology seemed to choke him. Suddenly he dived his hand in his pocket and let fly with a sharp heavy stone. It missed the girl and smashed a glass vase behind her, then he ran out like the wind. Canon Ritchie would have put the lad in reformatory if he could, but he was too late. The boy and his parents crossed over to Ireland that night and Craigneuk saw them no more.

I enjoyed life at St Pat's; once I discovered Dickens, and R. L. Stevenson, and Oliver Goldsmith I was as happy as a lark. The books were distributed daily for a full hour's lesson. There were other pupils, boys and girls, who delighted in them too. This so pleased one of the teachers, a Miss Morgan, that she built up a really good little library at her own expense. She was a good enthusiastic teacher but she got into trouble with the tough parents too, and one day a terrible looking woman burst in howling that her son Michael had been ill-treated. Actually the boy, a very chunky lump indeed, had been punished by Miss Muldoon. The very fragile Miss Morgan was a shaken young woman by the time the monster departed. I heard her say shudderingly to Mr Mo, 'I will forget her words, but her face, Dear God, never.'

I was shaken myself, for bang once more went my favourite illusion that all Irish women were gentle and soft-spoken like my mother.

At the end of that term there were two teachers with very opposite emotions; Miss Morgan would be happy to get rid of the chunky Michael, and Mr Mo would be dejected at the thought of bearing with him for the following year. It was his job to administer the final polish before we divided into the mines, ironworks, and steelworks. Poor man, how he persevered with his yearly crop of sow's ears.

Craigneuk was just as good a place for a kid to find fun as anywhere else in Scotland. We played football all the year round, we knew no close season and we had never heard tell of cricket; we stole strawberries from the fruit farms on the Clydeside; we bathed in the Calder River, and we played tig and hopscotch in the gaslit main street evenings. We stole empty bottles from the Beehive and we sold them back to it to get money to enter the geggies. That was the name for the travelling shows who set up their marquees and stayed as long as it was profitable. The fee was a penny for children and twopence for grown-ups. We patronised the ice cream palaces, they were the best lit, brightest, cleanest shops in the 'Neuk' and entirely run by Italians. It was in one of them that the Cowie Square Wanderers Football Club held their meetings; I was left half and club secretary.

We played on a strip of land divided from the back of the steelworks by a wire fence, and oh the joy of starting a match on a bright crispy, winter day! Our jerseys, when we managed to get some, were red, a compromise; the Irish section wouldn't wear the blue of Scotland, and the Scots wouldn't wear the green of Ireland. We didn't say it outwardly but we were delicately intercepting the implacable bigotry of our parents. A year or two later and it would seep through our systems too, some would adopt the Glasgow Rangers religion and like myself others would be steeped in the Glasgow Celtic religion.

To this day the Glasgow Rangers football club have never signed on a man who is a Roman Catholic. Glasgow Celtic are a trifle more broadminded, if the Protestants are good enough players then the Celts will have them. I remember them signing Billy Hogg, a non-Catholic and an ex-Ranger player, 'Ye kin hiv 'im,' sniffed our neighbour, Sanny Morton, 'He's only a hog anyway, efter this he'll be an Irish pig.'

Being an Irish Pig was something we at St Pats graduated to. While we were there we were promising sucklings, and once out in the world we showed 'em, or tried to. I can't say I tried very much myself, I left it to the spirited ones; myself, I was a shocking coward. The one time I all but broke from my craven spirit, proved me to be the complete coward. Myself and Paddy Murphy were set on by three Scots lads, one tackled the smaller Paddy, and two tackled me. I was anxious to shine in front of young Paddy, he was tough, confident, and rich. His parents ran a grocery store, his pockets were always filled with stolen sweets, and he actually came to school on a bike, the only one among us who could afford one.

I walloped away that day gloriously, and it pleased me even more to take punishment unflinchingly. I was right out of this world, the equal for once of fine tough fellows like young Paddy Murphy. As I slammed away, it encouraged me to hear cries for mercy coming from the other fight, and I told myself that Paddy had torn his opponent in two. I wasn't surprised, for Paddy I believed was terribly tough, come to think of it, so was I, and fit company for heroes. I snatched a moment to look across at the remains of young Murphy's opponent, and to receive my accolade, and maybe a bit of help in my own affair. To my horror it was Paddy who was howling, and the other fellow was doing the murdering.

My spirit crumbled like a handful of crushed biscuits, my opponents pummelled me till they were tired. The other one

let go Murphy so they could finish me off. When at last I
could scramble up my opponents had gone, and Murphy was
still lamenting. He made me so mad that I nearly refused a
bar of plain chocolate which he'd pinched from his old man's
store.

The Murphy family were the only Irish I knew who had
pulled themselves out of the pick and shovel range. Indeed
they hadn't travelled far, for the business was teetering on
the unsteadfast footing of a spear. I heard my father say so
to my mother, only not knowing Shakespeare he put it a
different way. For success Mr Murphy needed rid of two
things, one was young Paddy who stole half the stock, and the
other was Mrs Murphy who gave the other half away. She
had a kind heart and as most of the customers had no money
and consciences to match, the kind heart ticked while the
tick was mounting.

My mother was always a paying customer, and an occa-
sional ready money one after my father was promoted to
third-hand melter. More than once Mrs Murphy confided
to my mother that she would love young Paddy to study for
the cloth. He never did, not her way, but he did have an
affinity to cloth for later on he became a traveller in suit
lengths and silks. He was a real traveller too, for he ranged the
British Isles. His method was to buy cheap material in ware-
houses, wrap it in a piece of canvas, and then dressed in a
blue jersey, reefer jacket, and glazed peak cap, he traded in
the Irish clubs and pubs. He was always the sailor newly off
ship and giving away bargains in smuggled goods. Some fell
for it unknowingly, but others bought knowingly and willingly and with a certain admiration.

Paddy Murphy was only one of many operators in Scotland and Ireland; many of them originated in Crossmaglen, a
quiet little place not far from my parents home in Co
Armagh. Their activities were celebrated in song, 'Crossmaglen, where there's more rogues than honest men.'

But for the daily experience of jeers, and sometimes stones,
as we passed Craigneuk Public School, I could have imagined

I was at school in Ireland. Whether we were Ireland born, or first, second, or third generation Irish, we all boys and girls, had names like the map of Ireland. If the Protestant pupils of Craigneuk Public had to be believed, our faces were like the map of Ireland too. Not being brave made me seek allies past the Public school, and that was little trouble. All I did was lay in wait for Tommy McGuinness, Tommy Kelly, Peter Scullion, and Harry McInally. It preserved me physically and morally for there was safety in numbers, and a coward could pass muster in a crowd. Our fathers, all but one, worked on the steel furnaces; McInally's father was a coal miner. He was a brusher in the pit, I never knew what brushing consisted of, but he worked for a contractor. This person contracted out from the coal owners, employed and paid the men, and made a very good thing out of it.

There were contractors too on the steel works, and the workmen would have fared better without them. Their wages were paid in pubs instead of the works pay offices, and the contractors expected free drinks. In 1911 my Uncle Terry earned an average 5s. 6d. a day emptying wagons of brick, coal, and anthracite, for a contractor named Crosswood. That was very good money, for general labourers were earning 4s. 0d. a day, and railway platelayers were on about 19s. 0d. weekly. The contractor's gang were paid piecework and had to work very hard.

Harry McInally could hardly wait to grow up so that he could be a pitman like his dad. 'Yince I get the lang troosers on,' he said, 'I'll have money for the Tallies.' The Tallies he meant were the Italian ice-cream shops, and not the tally-men. They would come later when he grew up and was pro-viding for himself, and maybe a family. The tallymen pro-vided all the wearing apparel at our home, and in every home in Cowie Square. I suppose the good customers had to make up for the bad ones, but the tallyman got his money weekly at our door for years. We never grew rich enough to buy ready money. Craigneuk was so completely working class that my mother couldn't hope for real bargains in wearing apparel. There were no prosperous folk to do the needful at the jumble sales.

The menage, or household management scheme, was a great favourite with the women. They banded together to pay a weekly shilling towards a pound, or two pound total, and drew numbers for which week they would collect. The collector of the shillings was paid two shillings weekly for her trouble. At our house, like all the others, it meant boots for the children. When my brother and me needed the heavy nailed, Craigneuk styled boots my mother would form a menage and give herself number one draw.

The local name for the heavy boots was 'Tackity Bits'. The fathers wore them at work, and the kids wore them all the time, they lasted longer. My mother would have had the blacksmith shoe us, if it had been possible. In the summer we were easier on her, for we ran barefooted in school and out of it. Only the superior mother shod her child in summer. The rest of us had to do with a pair of trousers, no underpants, a shirt and jersey. Just the job for a lightning strip and a dive into the Calder River when school was over.

After the summer holidays in 1908 I moved into Mr Moreiety's class. I was eleven years old, coming on twelve at the time, and looked likely to remain there till school leaving time at fourteen years old.

Fairly frequently scholars were allowed to leave earlier in cases of domestic hardship. Harry McInally looked forward to this for his father had died of acute bronchitis, and he was the eldest of four. Already he was earning money selling evening newspapers. He was one of a band of boys who scooped up his bundle of papers at the railway station and scattered pell mell over the district. The quickest runner being the quickest sold out. I was a fellow newsvendor, and a good runner, and usually earned 1s. 9d. or so each week. Where mine went for pocket money Harry's went straight to his mother's purse. The coal pits which caused his father's premature death never had a more willing victim than Harry.

Each evening I finished my newspaper selling in a model

lodging house. It was a big unlovely place run by the Wishaw Burgh Council, and for men only. Tramps used it, and navvies passing through to other jobs also put up there. Most of the patrons were steelworks' labourers and stayed permanently.

They were not all hardliving, save for the fact that hard living had been thrust upon them. I was very friendly with one navvy type studious Irishman, and I looked forward to sharing a sausage often enough with him. Each man kept his food in a locker and cooked his meals on a communal hot-plate. My friend had travelled the roads and worked alongside Patrick McGill the Navvy Poet and he loaned me books of McGill's published work. One was, *A Navvy's Scrapbook*, another was verses about navvy life entitled, *Songs of the Dead End*. They were short, simple and interesting, and I couldn't know enough of the unusual navvy who wrote them. My model lodging house friend obliged me gladly. McGill was a Donegal man, and had left home at fourteen for the potato harvests of Scotland. He never went back to Donegal. In between jobs he sold his books from door to door, and in the pubs and dosshouses. He showed me a photograph of McGill and ever after I looked out for the man himself. I hoped to see him in the lodging house, but I never did.

Tommy Kelly was another classmate who quit school early, he too had to start providing when his father, a steel furnaceman, died. Mr Kelly was never a strong man, and there was no hope of thriving on his kind of job.

He was a 'Slasher In' on the furnaces. I didn't need to know of furnaces to realise that that was a crude strength-needing and strength-sapping occupation. His job was moving from furnace to furnace, where charging up was taking place. All the materials for steelmaking on the thirty-five-tons-capacity furnaces had to be thrown in by hand and shovel. The day of the electrical charging machines had dawned elsewhere, but not in Craigneuk. Mr Kelly and his mates helped shovel in the limestone, and throw in the pig iron, and steel scrap. When that was finished they rested until the next empty furnace required charging up. Between whiles he stoked his failing powers with whisky. It was no use, and now Mr Kelly, a very decent chap, was really resting at last in the Catholic portion of the cemetary outside Craigneuk.

Mr Moreiety parted with the two lads sympathetically, and could have used a bit of sympathy on himself when he viewed what was left of us. The girls were no trouble, he had a way with them, some of them would have mothered him, they were a hall head taller than he was. It was a rough core of porridge-fed nincompoops, just about three of them and a couple of fence-changing sycophants who bothered him. One of them was the chunky big chimp whose Maw had nearly wrecked Miss Morgan, and his ambition, no less, was to heave the little master in the air. To hold him over his head with upstretched arms, like he'd seen the strong men do when Lord John Sanger's circus visited Craigneuk. I never liked the fellow, I had a certain amount of fear for him, but I did tell him he'd need a lot more porridge before he could do that.

He must have mentioned his hopes to his Paw, for didn't he come along to demonstrate how to do it. He was a tall powerful man with a face as round and as intelligent as a turnip. Without a word he strode into the classroom, picked up the astonished Mr Moreiety and had him high in the air in no time at all. Then he let him down gently enough, dusted his hands, grinned happily at his proud son and swaggered out.

It was too much, Miss Muldoon summoned him for assault, and it cost him two pounds at Wishaw Burgh Police Court.

It was in Mr Moreiety's class that I really noticed how good-looking one or two of the girls were. It made me quite despondent when I noticed that they hadn't noticed how handsome I was. I didn't stand an earthly with them. I made up all sorts of smart sayings to impress them and then stuttered helplessly and incoherently when the chance came.

They always looked at me with pity and left me mentally kicking myself. What shook me most was suave Peter Scullion and Tommy McGuinness taking two of them out to practise waltzing when Mr Mo wasn't looking. I reckoned I had a legitimate grievance that they should know anything about waltzing, and that they should practise with real girls was deplorable.

I had better luck with Peggy Morton who lived in our close, I used to wait for her every Tuesday evening when she left a Band of Hope meeting. She was a very nice girl with just a shade of meekness which I liked, I felt at ease with it, it was the lively ones who showed up my deficiences. Things were going so well with Peggy and me that I even tolerated her father, her Paw, as she called him. This was really big of me for he was the one who hated the Glasgow Celtic football team; it showed the influence of sweet Peggy's love for me. I rather fancied an air of friendship too from Mr Morton until one day he stopped me in the close and told me quietly not to get too fond of Peggy. He had plans for her, and no Irish Catholic, especially one named Paddy, was included in them or ever would be.

I didn't act at all like a gallant lover, I was highly embarrassed and mumbled something and hurried away. I didn't say a word to Peggy about it, I didn't get a chance. I knew by the way she acted that her Paw had warned her too, when I saw her shooting past me I guessed that was her meek streak showing.

The Mortons moved into Glasgow a while afterwards and I never saw Peggy again. Mr Morton didn't live to see his plans fructify for he was killed at work three years after he left Craigneuk. Some years after that again I heard Peggy was married, and to an Irishman. Mr Morton would not have liked it.

One day I was sitting in class listening attentively to Mr Mo give forth in a history lesson, I liked history, it came after English as my favourite subject. The fellow sitting behind me was taking no interest at all, but was using my head as a shield for another activity. His name was Charlie Pearson and he was a solitary cove but well able to amuse himself. This time he had found a live gelignite cartridge and was working away with a penknife trying to make a whistle out of it. Luckily for me Charlie sought, and was granted permission to leave the class, there was no luck for Charlie for he came running in a moment or two later with three fingers blown off. It was months afterwards when I turned pale, I had just realised my fate if Charlie had stayed where he was.

After one full year in Mr Moreiety's I realised that I would have been better off in Motherwell Catholic Higher Grade School. There was still time after the holidays and on school resumption I went straight to Miss Muldoon for an entrance form. She showed little enthusiasm for my unexpected pursuit of higher education. 'You'll stay awhile', she said, 'and then you'll drift away like the rest of them. Why do you want to go?' I told her I had no desire for the boredom of a second year in the same class and she nodded understandingly. I didn't tell her my other big reason, that it pushed the threat of the steelworks in the background for a year or two longer. I had only a vague idea that a successful career at the higher grade might get me out of the threat of heavy industry altogether.

My parents were delighted at my decision, it was me and not them who had taken a lead in the matter. They were so far back in educational affairs that they took it for granted that St Pat's would be the beginning and end of anyone belonging to them. My mother had sufficient schooling to read her prayer book, and my father could make a fair effort to read a newspaper, that was all. That they were born to work was something they humbly and cheerfully accepted, that they had someone who might rise a little higher thrilled them.

The whole course at the higher grade school consisted of three classes, first year, second year, and third year. A successful career there qualified the boys to enter St Mungo's Academy in Glasgow. The very name St Mungo excited me,

and Academy was a good runner up. If I could actually get
there I felt that Miss Muldoon would have to change her
sour opinion of me, and I determined to be as good a scholar
as the next fellow. I knew that I hadn't the cleverness of some,
that had been proved to me at St Pat's. Others could play
around and still know their lessons but when I played
around I knew nothing. Application, and still more application was my only hope.

It wasn't long before I found out that Miss Muldoon knew
what she was talking about, for there were missing faces of both
boys and girls after the Christmas holidays. After the Easter
holidays three more girls quit and I wondered why. Why
should they leave when they were doing quite well? I supposed that finance was the trouble for we were a mixed lot
ranging from the very poorest to the fairly prosperous, and
from many districts. But later on I suspected another reason
for their departure. It occurred to me that three or four of the
better dressed girls were not bearing their prosperity too
graciously. Their queening around the recreation ground
arm in arm, and forever drawing a line between themselves
and the lower classes, had had effect. The girls from the
poverty stricken rows of Carfin, Cleland, and Craigneuk had
fled from this daily mortification.

I watched these young misses with great interest all during
my three years at the Higher grade. If they had class, they
didn't have scholarship, but that put no dent in their style.
They cut swaths of devotion from nearly every male in the
place. I worshipped from afar but without a hope, I was not
in their league.

Miss Muldoon's surly forecast of me had put me on my
mettle. I worked hard, and was in the prize list in my first
and second years. The prizes were awarded to the first ten
in the annual examination. Unfortunately I had a blind
side for maths, and in languages I needed very sympathetic
tutoring to reach even moderate success. I had that sort of
tutoring in my first two years until the French teacher left.
The one who took her place shot me to pieces.

She was a good looking woman of twenty five or so and possessed with the most sarcastic tongue in Scotland. Once I heard it whipcord into other pupils, I shivered. I felt I could never escape it. Although I was nearly fifteen at the time she scared me out of my wits, literally. I was as stupid as a mule in her presence, my heart jumped every time she looked near me. It wasn't long before I took my place in her gallery of dunces. Once in that, we might as well have walked out, she ignored us entirely. We were free from her tongue but we were outcasts. Across our homework she usually scribbled a scornful 'Rubbish', and would award us three marks out of one hundred. The marks she failed to put on my paper, she put on me; indelible ones.

All that time I was still dreadfully anxious to do well in the third-year exam. Fifty marks and over qualified to sit the entrance exam to St Mungo's. I would have liked that and worked tremendously hard in the other subjects to achieve it. In the end I failed and by only four marks. The French handicap was too much, for as usual I gained but three from the hundred. I don't think the teacher really disliked me, I puzzled her because I was good at other subjects and it made me a bit of a mystery to her. Since she couldn't solve the mystery she gave it up, and I was too frightened and in-articulate to help her.

It was the end for me, for I had no wish to spend another year there, not under such circumstances especially. It was some consolation that I left winning the gold medal award for Scripture. A year afterwards I heard she had married and I earnestly and silently wished her husband luck. I felt he needed it. Yet away from school, and from such aggrava-tions as me I daresay she was a pleasant young woman. I could think of no one who would look better nursing a baby. For its own sake I hoped the baby would have a handier grasp of the French language than I had.

5

The Beehive

Now that my schooldays were over the steelworks seemed inevitable to me. I had delayed my entry for eighteen months and I was getting on for my sixteenth birthday. I had little real objective when I first entered the higher grade, but I had acquired one there and failed to achieve it. I never explained the real cause of that failure to my parents. They saw how hard I had studied, they could hardly miss seeing me in our only room, and my friends passing outside saw me too. In the gaslit main street my shadow was visible as I pored over my books. I got credit for studying but little understanding for failing. My mother was cross, she had done her own little boasting of how her Patrick might even become a schoolteacher, and now here I was steelworks bound and eighteen months late at that. In her eyes I was somewhat like the spoiled priest that Irish Catholic mothers dread so much. In my mind I felt that way too.

My father, good man, said nothing, nor was he cross at all, he had little doubt of me doing my share of the world's work sooner or later. He was a first-hand melter then, still strong, still well, and still a fine-looking man, his wages were good but so was his thirst, and he didn't save much. My mother looked after him well and got him the best fillet steak from the good Scots butchers. They called it 'melter's steak' in Craigneuk for only the better paid steel furnacemen could afford it. She went to the good Scots bakers for her fancy stuff, we were as rich as that. All Scotland was proud of their butchers and bakers; years after the Scotsmen flocked to the steelworks in Corby, Northamptonshire, they

40

took their bakers and butchers with them.

But though my father was fit and well, he was forty-five now and he talked of steel-melting shops where machines charged the furnaces and where melters worked eight-hour shifts. He had no desire to leave the steel trade, he had reached the height of his ambitions, but he found the going still hard. His shirts were just as wet with sweat as ever they were. All her married life my mother had noted anxiously the state in which he arrived home. She knew the danger signals too well, the eyes far back in his head, the voice hoarse, almost inaudible, from his strength-sapped lungs. It was a poor place too for a man in such a state to come home to. A place of one room, with no bath, no hot water, and a lavatory at the end of the close which eight families shared. A gaslit home in a gaslit town where drunks often blew out the light and died in the night. It was quite true that we knew no other world, but now my father was hoping that there was a new world, where steel furnacemen even had gardens. He had heard of it from other melters and even though it meant starting all over again, it was still worth considering.

There were no gardens in Craigneuk, if there had been the bookmakers would have taken longer to get rich, and the pubs wouldn't have been so full. Nor would the fines and imprisonment at Wishaw Burgh Court been so frequent for breach of the peace, and for wife beating. Women in Craigneuk were often beaten by their husbands, and nearly always when their husbands were in drink. Often too the beatings took place in public houses. Not that the women accompanied their husbands to the pubs, for no woman in Craigneuk who valued her name would be seen in the long bars with their sawdusted floors and spittoons.

They got their beatings when the desperation of unpaid bills and hungry kids sent them in to drag out their poor foolish husbands. The husbands who were still in their dirty working clothes and with only the remnants of their pay packets left in their pockets.

The pubs were only drinking dens, every damn one of

them. They didn't need sprucing up because even as they stood they were still more inviting than the ugly homes, the owners feared no competition that way. They shut every Sunday so that the landlords could count their gold, and they all bore the supreme insult, 'No Women Allowed.'

If the women had only known they would have flocked in and refined the dismal holes. They should have taken their pleasure with their husbands and all come out sober and contented like people did in other parts of Britain. But that was much in the future and what was more immediate was me starting to earn my living. I became third barman and general knockabout in the Beehive Bar, and although it was very near the steelworks, it was still outside the main gates and that suited me fine.

The pub opened according to law at eight o'clock in the mornings and remained so until ten in the evenings. To make sure it was in good order for the customers we arrived at seven-forty-five, and the washing up and sweeping up delayed us to after ten-thirty at night. Altogether a fifteen hours daily affair but only really busy at week-ends. The colliers stirred things up when they drew their wages on the Fridays, and our real bonanza arrived when the steelworkers were paid on Saturdays. It was believed that the pubs shut on Sundays because the authorities hoped the boozers might repent and go to church. But many of them instead went to shebeens, mostly run in private houses where the worst whisky was sold at high prices. There were others who did go to church and I used to see many of the Beehive patrons at mass in St Patrick's on the Sunday mornings. Some of the big spenders of the night before looked real bad too, and I often wondered if the Lord would blame me for it. Like my mother I was very religious, and she, like most Irish peasant Catholics, couldn't answer many questions on it, but for her it was the old sustainer, the thing that made Craigneuk bearable.

I was certain that the Lord wouldn't blame me for making a fortune from the drink traffic for my wages were only twelve bob a week, that ran less than twopence an hour for a ninety-hours stretch. Still I had a free half-day, but only when the boss had ran out of excuses to prevent it. I missed my football very much: I was good at it and had played for my school in representative matches.

The Beehive was a nondescript place and it looked as old as the hills even then. I had passed it most days of my life but I had never remembered it being freshly painted. Still I wouldn't have noticed anyway unless a can of paint fell on me. There were two other barmen besides me and a manager. The owner, a very rich Irish widow, lived somewhere near Glasgow. She owned other bars in the city and so did many other Irish people, in fact the Irish had a firm grip on each side of the counters.

The manager was a tiny middle-aged Scot named Geordie McKie, it was he who engaged me and in doing so he was following his usual practice of employing Roman Catholics. Irish employees pleased the very large group of Irish customers, and the Catholic part of it pleased Geordie. He was a cynical little heathen himself but he firmly believed that religious training at home and in school made honest men. Not only honest but obedient as well. Too honest to steal his money, and obedient enough to steal the customers.

So small a man seemed out of place managing so tough a pub, but only if one didn't know him. Actually he was famed for his ability to handle the most awkward of customers. He could rely on good aid from Hughie Clark the head barman. Clark was a natty young fellow only twenty-one years old, and a fair professional boxer. He would have been more of a professional and less of a barman, but for his desire to preserve his very good looks. He was a dancing man and there was a frequent procession of young ladies diving into the outdoor department to talk to him.

Hughie had a very grim streak in him and he lashed out very quickly at any awkward customer. He used them as training sessions for his ring fights. He was far too handy with his fearsome fists and it was as plain as could be what the end would be when he lashed out. Once he picked a quarrel with a rough-looking man who must have been forty years old. The fellow wasn't drunk and was bothering no one until Hughie started. In no time at all he was out on his ear. I was so enraged I forgot my usual cowardice and put my fists up to him. He grinned and said, 'Come back in four or five years when you've grown up.' I was as tall as he was, although I wasn't quite sixteen.

The second barman, Willie Ferris, lived in the same close as me. He was twenty years old and hadn't too strong a constitution, but with a tremendous cheerfulness. He fell out with no one, and he was the confidant of many customers when anything bothered them. When they got into trouble through drinking too much in the Beehive, Willie went to court to help pay the fines. Little Geordie didn't like parting with money, but he often fell for Willie's, 'He has a wife and family, jail him and his job's gone and we've lost a customer, so you put up the twenty-five bob and I'll spring the other dollar.'

Once, contrary to business instincts, Willie advised a customer to go teetotal; the chap tried hard and used to report progress over a bottle of ginger ale. 'Drink it somewhere else,' advised Willie, 'Pubs are dangerous places.' We didn't see the man again until the Glasgow Fair holidays; he called in to tell us that he was, 'Awa' doon the watter wi' the wife and bairns.' His wife and three excited children were outside waiting to set off for the first holiday in their lives. Willie didn't realise the wonderful thing he had helped to bring off.

The oddballs who frequented the 'Hive' delighted Ferris hugely. He collected their sayings and sent his scouts after them when they lacked the price of a 'let'. The word stood for entrance money and three half pence was enough, the price of a gill of beer. Once inside who knew what big butter and egg man might call drinks up for the house.

Day after day, week after week, the pub was suiting me fine. Each morning I donned a heavy waterproof apron and set into the chores. There were brasses to polish, fresh sawdust to lay, empties to wash and to refill, and windows to clean. After all that it was lunchtime, and that was a movable feast, for I never went home until the chores were over. I reserved the rest of the day in donning the white apron of the Scottish barman.

I fancied myself in that white apron and my mother kept it snow-white, like she did my father's sweat towels. I loved the week-days best of all, they were quiet, with the best sort of customers calling, and the conversations often excellent. Those customers were the high ups of the district, they had money while the payday whooper ups were broke. After payday the steel melters mostly went on strap, they ran up fairly high bills too, as much as thirty shillings a week. But they all paid up promptly and tipped the barmen.

Giving credit was against the law and had to be done quietly. That suited the melters too; they had no wish to let the lesser fry see they were broke. The procedure was always the same; a man would choose a quiet spot at the bar, order his drink and hand me a coin. I would hand him back change for a half crown or a half sovereign if he wished it. But the coin he proffered would only have been a penny or a halfpenny. Little Geordie knew all about it, but he never mentioned it, he trusted his Irish Catholic barmen to do the correct thing.

Geordie was as keen as Canon Ritchie, the Highland Scot in charge of St Pat's, that we should go to church regularly. A lax Catholic might have rifled the till.

The Beehive had one long bar that stretched from the swing doors to the far wall. It was not straight but curved at the top end where any one standing there could see everything that was going on. There were only two very small rooms where customers could sit if they wished. Very few bothered to do so, they preferred leaning against the bar, drinking and smoking and spitting in the sawdust, you know, Western style. They looked tough too but only on Saturdays; the poverty of the week-days tamed them but when their pay packets were full they were real Jesse James' sans mustangs.

I wasn't sure if I liked the Saturdays at all. It was life, busy, throbbing, raw, and thrilling; and disturbing. When we were ejecting poor drunken fools still in their steelworks muck at closing time, I hated it. I disliked the manager showing me the tricks of the trade and expecting me to practise them. I saw no reason for it, I was giving him plenty of time for two pence an hour, and that I thought was enough without cheating people as well. I was all for honesty, it kept my mind at rest, and made the job easier when I went to monthly confession at St Pat's. Confessing my sins wasn't simple for me; somehow my breathing troubled me as soon as I entered the small confessional, and claustrophobia wasn't the cause of it.

However, there were certain adjustments to be made in my tender conscience, there were certain relaxations I allowed myself else I would have been a saint entirely, a very hungry one too. I simply had to scrap my scruples when it came to the biscuits and cheese stand. They were on a large plate with a glass cover and they were almost safe from mankind until I came along. Soon the grocer, a door or two away, had a regular order for replenishments. He wondered if navvies had started taking meals in the pub.

Cigarettes too received my attention. I was a non-smoker when starting in the 'Hive' and I was a confirmed smoker when I left it. I wasn't always the confirmed payer, they were too handy on the pub's shelves, but I made a fair effort.

I never touched the liquor, neither the short stuff or the ales. I'd have preferred dishwater. I made up for it somewhat on the minerals, I found they went nicely with the biscuits and cheese.

One Saturday the Irishmen held a gala day in Craigneuk. The boss was rubbing his hands in glee when he first heard of it, for ours was the nearest pub. We were all prepared for a gala day too. All day long the Irishmen crowded the bar. Most of them wore green sashes and cocked hats and belligerent looks, as if they were listening for the sound of a Scotch accent. They didn't hear any; only the accents of Connaught and Ulster floated around. One look at them and our real Scots customers went elsewhere to quench their thirsts. Even little Geordie, who feared no one, made a brave attempt at an Irish accent.

We sold whisky by the bucket-ful, and real firewater it was too. A specially bad whisky at a specially big price. All day long we expected trouble, but never a cheep of it came from the customers. Just good hard drinking and in the best of tempers. The little manager was as pleased as punch that evening as he wallowed in the takings. If those big men had only known how he diddled them, what would have happened to little Geordie? He was only the size of a leprechaun any way, a real tom thumb of a man. But he was all right, a nervy, dapper fellow, whose courage was something I very much lacked.

The one miscalculation the boss made was in the meat pie department. We had one hundred small ones ready, but our customers ate only twenty of them. I had been too busy to snaffle any for myself. The place being shut on Sunday, I couldn't get at them. I made up for it on the Monday, for they were still palatable. That evening there were still many left and I hated to see them waste, so I filled the baskets of our lady customers. They came into the off department for their husband's half pints. Just near finishing time the boss fancied one himself. It didn't give him indigestion, because he didn't get one, there was none left.

He looked very hard at me and I started thinking of the bad whisky we sold to the Irishmen. Maybe he did too, for he left it at that. Before we quit I heard him tell a customer that I had eaten eighty meat pies. That was an exaggeration, for I only ate ten. Being a Scotsman little Geordie never imagined I'd given any away.

It was always a great relief to finish on Saturday nights. Sometimes it would be well after eleven and I'd really be tired. Often too I was emotionally upset by the brawling of drunken aggressive men. Fear, sadness, pity would be all mixed up in my head. Though by a miracle of temperament my own home had escaped it, it never struck me that life needn't be so ugly.

My mother would be waiting when I reached home, ready to give me my big supper and to listen to some pub gossip. She'd never been in the bar proper of the 'Hive' but she knew all the staff and plenty of the customers. She wasn't a teetotaller, in a later age she would have enjoyed a pub evening with her husband. As it was, she made do with the bottle of stout my father brought home for her. My sister Anna Mary would be in bed and my brother Peter would be out somewhere with his footballing pals. He was a very good player and kept it up after he went on the steelworks rolling mills.

It was a certainty that my father, if he was free of work, would be in Glasgow on Saturday evenings. He always arrived home on the last train, always sober, and laden with purchases from the Glasgow Market. He loved the bustle of open air markets, and the grafters working in their naptha-lit stalls. I loved it too, and many a time I went with him before I started work in the pub. Once a keenfaced, well dressed young grafter employed me for an afternoon. My job was holding up his naptha lamp in the dim winter weather while he sold his cheap jewellery from a small leather bag on the ground. My father felt I was happy enough and had gone for one of his long walks through the wilds of Bridgeton, where the big Highland policemen patrolled the pavements three at a time and even in the day light that way.

My employer's trade fascinated me, first he demonstrated his packets of 'Alaskan & Parisien Gold' and then sold them like lightning at a shilling a time. His till was the lid of his open case and I tried hard each time to count his takings as I stood with my naptha flare. Each sortie of selling was well within an hour's duration. When he tired he quit, thanked his patrons; scooped his money up; shut his case which held hundreds of packets; gave me sixpence for a meat pie and disappeared somewhere for a while. Then again he whipped up a crowd with his sparkling tongue and stock, filled the case lid with shillings again, and retired once more. He gave me a half crown for my trouble, and a fascinating insight into a facet of market life.

With my supper over, my wages handed to my mother, and my half-crown pocket money in my fist, I would grab my cap and belt as hard as I could to the nearest ice cream palace. I'd walk up to the counter and order a slider, that meant ice-cream between two sponge biscuits. Once finished, I'd repeat the order twice over, and be left with two shillings. Then I'd tuck into the Clown machine at the end of the counter. It was the forerunner of the fruit machines of a later day, only more modest; it accepted pennies and the prizes were threepenny checks to be spent at the counter. Sometimes I'd have a handful of checks, but more often I'd be flat broke within twenty minutes.

Then out again, but not home; midnight would be well past, but I was a worker entitled to my play. I would walk the pavements right into Motherwell town, and turn at the town cross, down Merry Street, heaven knows what comedian named it that, into Windmillhill Street and on the road home again. All I would meet would be drunks, still winging their petulant, pathetic way home, to break the hearts of some poor women by the very sight of them. They were by no means all customers of the Beehive, there were plenty more pubs besides that, but those poor critters always gave me a guilty feeling. As if I'd set out deliberately to make them drunk for the sake of a profit. It seldom occurred to me that I was even more broke than they were. Once returned I would stand at the close, bidding goodbye to the departed week and wondering if I could scrounge threepence from my mother later in the day. I needed a penny or two to put on the plate at eleven o'clock mass in St Patrick's.

My weekly half-day often provided my real taste of high life, second-hand of course, for with me it had to be free. There was always a big dance taking place within travelling distance of my feet. I used to go outside the hall watching the handsome gentlemen hand their lovely ladies from their hired-horse-cabs. The door was as far as ever I got, for I lacked the girl and the know-how, as well as the money.

It was the custom then to watch the arrivals, just like people watch the arrivals at film premieres today. Some watched with pleasure, some wanted a laugh, and some watched with some sadness mixed in their interest. There were always some young mothers among the crowds, and late as it would be, they'd have babies in the long shawls, and one or two more clinging to their skirts. Their own span of carefree happiness must have been short, if it had ever started at all.

Often my own feeling was awe, when I saw some dunderheaded ex-school-mate hand out his girl like the best of them. He'd only be sixteen or so like me, and I couldn't understand how he had reached such heights. The ball would go on through the night, until five the next morning. All the young bloods would be making a devil of a show in their blue serge suits, white silk shirts, and black silk ties. None of them ever looked better than my head barman Hughie Clark. He was indeed a bonnie laddie, as the Scots express it so well. Always too he had the loveliest girl of them all. One in particular I remembered for ever, she was so young and so fresh, with the pink of her cheeks matched by her charming frock. As she stood with her magnificent shetland wool shawl loosely over her shoulders she was breathtaking in her beauty. I would have given a year of my young life to have been in Hughie's place that night.

It was a day or two after when he spoke of her to me. 'She's Maggie Durrane,' he answered my query, 'She's a bottle washer at Nimmo's place in Wishaw. A real nice wee lassie,' he finished affectionately.

I never saw her again, or maybe I didn't recognise her when the magic had gone, but she was a bonnie, bonnie lassie that night.

I was never at ease in a dance hall. The ones I attended found me tongue-tied, nervous, and leaden-footed. Around me would be fellows I knew well and they'd be waltzing

6

The Characters in the 'Hive'

I was nicely established in the Beehive when Craigneuk opened its first music hall cum cinema. Up to then all we had for entertainment were the travelling geggies and makeshift halls showing moving pictures. When we wished to see a live show we went to the New Century theatre in Motherwell, or to the music halls in Wishaw or Hamilton. Now we had our own and better still, since the Beehive displayed its show-bills, there was a free pass to be had. There was only Willie Ferris and me for that, for Hughie the head barman had his dignity to think of. I wasn't so particular, it was the only way I could get in.

Little Geordie the boss held the major shares in the venture, and the artistes spent much time in the bar drinking whisky, and on account too. Geordie put a stop to that for he soon found out that the majority were of no account. The hard up ones used to sleep in the hall at night; they were poor but honest, the dishonest ones often bilked the Craigneuk land-ladies.

I found it very hard to refuse credit to the theatricals. T_ intrigued me, for they were so right out of my wo_ much so that I didn't mind paying for my inter_ little of the firm's stock. When it hurt my consc_ to think of the rot-gut whisky I had served to t'_ gala day, and somehow that seemed to mak_

In the first winter of the new hall we h_ was terrible stuff, and the word wer_ artistes were so hard hit that they _ but the people had to feed them _

gracefully, expertly, reversing nonchalantly
gods. They'd lead their happy partners from
the dance was over, chatting and laughing
gaily. How the devil did they manage it? The
same as me, their parents had come out of an
as mine had. No one had taught them any so
home, for like my home no one knew any. Again
like my home, weren't big enough to swing a cat i
a great mystery, but I never breathed it out loud.
on pretending I was one of the boys.

the third week there was an audience of three, and the following night there were three less. We kept on feeding them and opened a subscription list to send them to their homes. Willie Ferris and myself as a willing helper had them away with railway tickets and a couple of pounds each in their pockets. They all lived in England and there were nine of them, so the Craigneuk people did very well.

I had my own pet member of that company. He was an old man of great dignity and a very beautiful complexion; he claimed the secret for it was plenty milk applied outwardly. What he applied inwardly was my secret; I had to conjure up the image of the gala day quite often. Not only liquor, he needed cigarettes and bread and cheese too. My mother gave him money almost daily and felt well repaid by the tales of his theatrical lifetime. She too, even more than me, was starved of a little variety, she really loved too to be addressed as 'My dear lady.' It was a change from my father's, 'Hey, Mary Ann.'

The manager of the hall was a fine young fellow about thirty and very fond of whisky. I knew that for I had the job of collecting the empties from his cubbyhole of an office. I knew too that his salary was £150 a year, and that wasn't enough for his thirst. It didn't seem to be very joyous drinking, for each week he grew a little sadder. I regretted it too, for he was a kindly man and very considerate to a shy creature as I was then. He met a tragic end on the railway line in Motherwell station. I never heard whether he had a wife or family, or any relatives at all. He was just a decent sort of fellow that I knew slightly and regretted a lot.

I only met the lady who owned the pub once. It was an easy afternoon with no customers, and I was standing at the door having a look at Craigneuk, when she came from nowhere. 'Have you nothing better to do,' she asked sharply, and passed into little Geordie's small office. She stayed an hour discussing business with him, and when she came out I had something better to do, I was polishing glasses. This time she smiled and handed me a five shilling piece and told me to be a good boy. It was the biggest coin, and the biggest sum of money, I had ever owned.

I was free on the following afternoon and I went to Wishaw Pavilion to hear Lily Morris sing, 'Don't have any more, Mrs Moore.' Afterwards I ate ice cream and watched Miss Morris enter the Pavilion bar with her pianist. I then had a fish and chip supper and bought chocolate bars. After that I hopped on a tramcar for home. Once there my mother put down my good supper which naturally I was ready for. I gave her a shilling I owed her, which shook her, it had never happened before. I also gave her a bar of chocolate, and the same plus a sixpence each to my brother and sister. After all that I had change left over.

I grew as fond of the 'Hive' characters as Willie Ferris himself, and like him I got on famously with them. They opened out with us where they were chary of Hughie Clark. He was a little above the dead-end customers and quick with the rough edge of his tongue, also they had seen his terrible fists in action. Willie and me were different, we were simple souls with the great natural wisdom to perceive the grain of gold in the despised ones. We had generous hearts too even if it was other folks property we were dispensing. I was finding out that I liked people, and the knowledge was heartening. One man I liked was the Fiddler Smith who lived in Dymoch's Buildings just opposite the pub, and a very dreary hole indeed. When the Fiddler's funds were punctured Willie would whistle for him and he would be over like a hound dog. There would be a pint of beer ready on the counter for him, drippings from the tap but good, and with a nice head on it. Once he got inside, who knew what good luck might befall the Fiddler; maybe a steelworks head roller or a mine contractor would call for drinks to the house. It wouldn't cost a fortune, the donor would see that in a flash, and the effort would put an extra polish on his legendary crown.

Entering a favourite pub can make any man thoughtful at times. Who will be in? Who will come in? Can I stand my

corner? are all serious questions now and again. With the
Fiddler the only question was, How the devil can I get in? In
really desperate times when all good patrons were either
dead or broke, the Fiddler would throw all decency aside and
hurry in seeking only a light for his pipe. Since the pipe
would be as empty as his pocket it wasn't much use him
puffing away, but his eyes would be everywhere and his
ears cocked for the good word. Very often there was no good
word, especially when Hughie Clark was around; then he
would shuffle out with contumely pouring on his hardened
head.

The Fiddler was a lugubrious cut of a fellow of fifty or so.
He was very shortsighted and he wore a pair of rimless
spectacles. These, added to his faded swallow-tailed coat and
dickie shirt front and collar combined, gave him an air of
appalling gentility. His large drooping moustache came out
frothily every time he pulled at a pint. Willie claimed that he
wrung it out in lean spells. No one ever heard him play a
fiddle, but he had one all right and a very dilapidated thing
it was. To see the Fiddler with his instrument under his arm
always reminded me of the castle ghost, the one whose
appearance heralded tragedy. It only appeared when the
monetary situation was really desperate. At such times the
Fiddler would sidle down the street and head for Wishaw
town, a mile away. Once there he'd make for one of the
poorest streets and stand fiddle in hand, cap on the ground,
as if he had just finished a fine piece, and was waiting for the
well-earned gravy. There must have been kind patrons, for
he always paid for his beer in halfpennies when he entered
the pub afterwards.

The Fiddler never smiled, not facially anyway, but intern-
ally he enjoyed his own little jokes. I remember four wise-
acres making no protest when he told them that America was
discovered when Columbus released two doves from his ship
and one came back chewing gum.

The most inoffensive customer we had was Francey Milord.
He was a gaffer on the steelworks in charge of a labouring

gang. It wasn't much of a job, and paid about thirty shillings weekly, but it meant status. Francey could don the blue gutty collar of the upper classes. He was a middle-aged bachelor and lived with a widowed sister, and his nickname, although derisive, was congratulatory too, for he was spotless in dress, demeanour, and language. He was the only man in Craigneuk to use a nail file instead of his teeth when trimming his fingernails, and his linen stood out in a district of cloth caps and mufflers. He knew his nickname and liked it too, though none of us called him milord to his face. It took a brave man to wear a bowler hat in Craigneuk, but Francey did. He swung a neat curve too with his silver topped cane.

Francey was careful with money and his habits were precise; every evening at nine o'clock he drank a pint of beer, threepence. He always paid with a small threepenny piece, he treated no one and sought none. That was fair enough but it annoyed Hughie Clark and he started saving up Francey's threepenny pieces. He hoped sometimes he would run short of them and offer a pound instead. When at last it did happen and Francey proffered a gold sovereign, Hughie dumped down seventy nine three penny bits. 'I've been saving these up for you,' he unsmilingly remarked. Francey scooped them up and like a true aristocrat murmured, 'Very good, Mr Clark, I shall return them at my leisure.' He did too; it took seventy-nine days.

Francey had a great admirer in Celtic McGurk, though sartorially Celtic was a mess. He had only the one suit for work, and play, and he was a football fanatic. He was a shunter on the steelworks, a pughunter was the Craigneuk word for that job, and he only lived for the Saturday afternoons. Matchdays he recognised by turning his muffler inside out, and buying a new clay pipe. Then in the evenings he discussed the highlights at the Beehive. He was a dark complexioned man about forty five with a guttural voice, and very much like a Lithuanian. I noticed he always moved up to Francey to discuss the game, which was a one-sided affair, for Milord knew nothing about football. He just kept nodding his head politely, and wished Celtic would go away. Celtic kept it up for weeks, gabbling away with his pipe in his mouth. Then suddenly he bothered the little man no more, and I was curious to know why. 'He's a nice wee man,' he told me, 'but I didna jaloose that he is deef.' So I put the question to Francey, 'A pleasant enough fellow.' he answered, 'but I don't speak Lithuanian.' I never made them any the wiser; they were poles apart anyway.

During my time in the 'Hive' three important things happened. The opening hour changed from eight o'clock to ten o'clock, my wages rose from twelve shillings to fourteen shillings, and beer went up from three to fourpence a pint. I was indifferent about the price of beer, I felt no richer with my pay increase, but I thought opening at ten was the life of Riley. It was civilization not to rise until nine o'clock, and very few adults in the 'Neuk' enjoyed the privilege.

Actually I had only experienced one spell of really early rising and I had a very poor opinion of it. It was a year or two before I quit school, and I had taken over from a newspaper seller at the steelworks main gate, while he recovered from bronchitis. It was winter time, and I had to be up at five and out to the railway station to collect the newspapers, and make my sales to the day-turn men. Once they were served I had to hang around until the last of the nightshift men came out about seven-thirty. All the time I was half asleep and blue with the cold and only three bob richer at the week-ends. I almost preferred the bronchitis myself.

The 'Neuk' looked dismal at the best of times, but at that early hour it was awful. There was nothing but sad silent figures, dressed in the almost uniform garb of shabby overcoats, mufflers, cloth caps and heavy nailed boots. The Beehive was heaven, comparatively, and although I met some customers in their wildest and most foolish moments I met them often in their finest moments too. The fellow shivering his sad early way to the steelworks was a different fellow behind his pint in the Beehive. I had some good fun and some great interest in listening to life and its living as I polished away at the glasses. The boss liked them shining and I did too, so like my mother with her knitting I talked as I worked. I'd grown very fond of the shabby old pub, and every push of its swing doors brought me a chance of some interesting personality.

Many of our patrons were Poles and Lithuanians, and, like the Irish, most of them were Roman Catholics. To the Scots and to the Irish alike they had all the one title, Johnny Pole. Their unpronounceable names disappeared, after a generation or two had passed through St Patrick's school. The teachers and fellow pupils put an Irish twist to them and even added an O or a Mac here and there. As a consequence, there may be fellows in Craigneuk today fondly talking of the Irish grandparents, when they really mean their Polish grandparents.

The police, who always had a busy time in Craigneuk, sometimes used the Johnny Poles to cover up their own blunders. There was one Saturday evening when a Polish customer, perfectly sober and inoffensive, stepped out of the 'Hive' and found himself spreadeagled on the police barrow. The man the police really meant to arrest had been smuggled away by friends, and to save their face they needed a substitute. The Pole spent the week-end in the police barracks and was fined thirty shillings for being drunk and incapable. The two policemen had the grace to pay the fine, they also had the cheek to warn the victim on the danger of entering public houses. I suppose the Pole, if he understood them at all, would think there was more danger in leaving public houses.

During the week-days trade always sparked up a bit in the last hour. It is a favourite time in publand everywhere. The steel melters on nightshift used to call in for a last strengthener on their way back after supper. There would be another nine hours in front of them, and many a time, especially in summer, they looked done up as it was. I used to look out for my father when he worked nightshift, and pull his drink as soon as he entered the swing door. A glass of whisky and a pint of beer was his working drink, and he followed it up with a schooner of beer to top it off. If it was warm weather his blue flannel shirt would be open at the neck and his sweat towel tucked into his leather belt just over his hip pocket. Sometimes, in his hurry to reach the 'Hive' before closing time, his blue furnace glasses would still be resting over his left ear. There was nothing unusual about all this to the Craigneuk people, for heavy industry dominated the place and its slaves were acting true to character.

Sometimes my father came in with a countryman of his named Luke Sherry. He was a furnaceman too, but slowed down with the weight of fifty-four years spent mostly in steelworks, ironworks, navvying jobs, and the harvest fields of Scotland and England. My father's life was a replica of his, for they had been almost constant companions from my father first leaving home. He was fourteen at the time, Luke was twenty-two, and both were in the same squad of potato diggers on a farm in Berwickshire.

The potatoes were all lifted with forks; mechanical diggers may or may not have been invented then. The Scots farmers would not have used them anyway, for they are very canny. They still are shrewd people and I doubt if mechanical diggers are in vogue to this day on the border farms. They slice too many potatoes for the farmers' liking. Besides, the hardy, experienced Donegal potato harvesters who still go over every year, are almost machines themselves. Their tireless use of the fork, their gentle upturning of every potato with the end prong, is a treat to watch.

Luke Sherry, in my Beehive days, was a first-hand melter who could no longer stand up to the manual labour involved on a hand-charging cold metal melting shop. With the firm's knowledge he paid a man to do the work for him. Luke only concentrating on the care of his furnace and its contents. In a mild way it was a reminder of the contract system which operated on steel melting shops and rolling mills only a few years before that. The contractors paid the men at the usual day rates, and could come away with fifty and sixty pounds weekly for themselves.

They were highly skilled, experienced men, but they grew into such great gentlemen, attending race meetings and even owning racehorses, that their poorly paid workmen revolted. The managements themselves were slow to realise how advantageous it would be to get rid of the contracting system. The Steel Melters Union, of which my father and Luke Sherry were members, fought for a long time, and in vain, to have things altered. Then something happened at Blochair steelworks near Glasgow to make Mr Riley the general manager think hard. The firm had put down thousands of pounds of advanced rolling mill stock but were not getting the output which had been confidently expected. So Mr Riley sought the advice of John Hodge, who was a steel melter, and who was also the founder and general secretary of the Steel Melters Union.

Hodge's advice was clear, 'Your millmen,' he said, 'are poorly paid datal workers, while the contractor sits back and takes the cream. Get rid of him, put the men on a basic rate, with a bonus for output, and see what happens.' Riley did so and the output went up 200 per cent. He played fair and didn't reduce the rates. From then onwards the contracting system gradually faded away in steelworks.

Hodge started his trade union in 1886 and he made a very good job of it. It is incorporated now in the Iron & Steel Confederation. He wasn't alone, of course, but his canny Scots common sense helped to lay the foundation of the wise, arbitrary, collective bargaining system which steelmen and steelmasters pursue.

The system of the 'Gaffer's Furnace' was also abolished because of the Union's efforts. With this system the samplepasser was paid by the melters instead of the firm. The samplepassers always chose the highest producing furnace which, of course, paid the best wages. The men on the furnace being relegated one grade down to make room for him.

In 1904 the Steel Melters Union and the steelmasters

agreed to a Wages Sliding Scale method of payment. A standard rate was fixed which could not be altered except in changed conditions, and the wages rose and fell according to the production and the price of steel. Gradually the system covered all branches of steel production and satisfied every one for more than thirty years. The second world war necessitated changes, and the system has not yet been resumed.

So far as I know my father never worked in a non-union melting shop, but Luke Sherry worked in the Mossend steel-works when it was non-union. The works was only a few miles from Craigneuk and it was the last stronghold of the old conservative union-hating employers. Luke was there in 1907 and he had to sign a form stating that he would not join a trade union. This was about Mossend's last kick at trade unionism, for the steel melters were persuaded by the Steel Melters Union organiser to join up in spite of the firm. The organiser, whose name was Jimmy Walker, soon gained them the same advantages which were prevalent in other melting shops.

I often saw Jimmy Walker in the Craigneuk main street, always accompanied by steel melters, and always off to meet the melting shop manager and try settle some grievance or other. The branch meetings were held in private houses and very often some sneak told what had transpired to the melting shop manager. This man would victimise the householder by suspending him on some trivial grounds. It was Walker's job to get the suspension removed. My father, a quiet, tongue-tied man when at a meeting, had a great admiration for the determined and loquacious Walker. Years later he became a Labour M.P. and was killed crossing a street in the London wartime blackout.

One evening my father came in the pub about six o'clock. I was surprised to see him at that hour, for he was on night-shift and started work only an hour before it. He was still in working clothes with his very white sweat towel advertising my mother's capable laundering. I was more interested than bothered, until he stayed long enough to take more drink than I had ever served him before. It was moody drinking, too, and suspecting the cause of it I asked him what was wrong. My suspicion was dead right; he had been suspended from work because a mishap had occurred on his furnace. He had been blamed for it although the mishap happened six hours after he left the works.

7

The Steelworks

My father was suspended from work for one week and he was very unhappy about it. The bath of his furnace, wherein the liquid metal lay, had given way and the metal had poured out on the floor. It had been a scene of chaos as the sparkling mass tore its devouring way, and the sweating melters had shovelled banks of dolomite to divert it. It was cleared away afterwards when it solidified and cooled, and would go back in the furnace to be re-melted.

Since my father had been responsible for the repair of the furnace bath he alone was suspended. It was considered that he had failed in his duty to make the bath solid enough to bear the metal charged into it. So far as he was aware he had performed his duty with the same efficiency as any other time. When the furnace had discharged its metal he and the other melters had shovelled in the dolomite used for such occasions. They had filled in every worn part and taken time to do the job properly. He could swear to that, but the element of chance, good or bad, was always in steelmaking at that time. He had been unlucky and there was nothing he could do about it.

He told me there was no victimisation, that suspensions for serious mishaps were a recognised procedure in the trade, and that Jimmy Walker's presence was not required. He didn't feel guilty of slipshod work and the management didn't say that was so. My father had gone into the manager's office accompanied by the branch union representative, a man named Tommy Weir, Tommy was a second-hand melter on the opposite shift to my father, and had once suffered suspension himself. 'It's the luck of the draw, Peter,' he told my father over a pint in the Beehive, 'When things like that happen the shop manager has to prove to the top management that he is alert and doing his job.'

My father agreed that was true, but that it was little consolation. It was bad enough, he said, to lose a week's pay but that wasn't the whole of it.

Later on I asked my father what he meant, and he told me that suspension ruined a man's confidence, and without that his judgment of heat and the condition of his charge was impaired. Suspension, he claimed, turned a melter into a bundle of nerves and hesitations; it made his working hours a misery, and would remain that way for a long time afterwards.

My father was right. I found that out for myself years later. The suspension system was alive in British steelmaking up to the start of the second world war. It can hardly be alive anywhere today, for life and work has changed very much since then. It was not so much a vindictive policy as a mistaken one, for successful steelmaking was even more a frame of mind than a job of work, and suspension put the right frame right out of a man's mind.

I remember one melting shop manager who looked forward to the bad old days returning after the second world war was over. He had a lot of spite to work off and he was fond of whipcracking. He lived long enough to wonder how he had been so foolish. There was no going back in steelmaking and a jolly good job that we didn't.

One good result from my father's misfortune was that my mother, to cheer him up, suggested the family spend a day at Loch Lomond: so I took a day from work, with the boss's consent, and we all sailed from the Broomilaw in Glasgow to the bonny, bonny banks of Loch Lomond. We were astonished that such loveliness should be but an hour or so from the wilds of Glasgow. I was surprised that it was in Scotland at all, for I had visualised the country to be one vast expanse of steelworks, ironworks, and coalmines. It was the first time any of us had visited a Scottish beauty spot. We knew that what 'doon the watter' meant, but we had never experienced it.

It was an old Scots engineer who told me of the sailings from the Broomilaw. He was a Beehive patron, a lone drinker, and he took a lot of it, but he always left on his feet and always bid me farewell the same way, 'You're a bonny laddie, but you're Irish,' and off he would go shaking his head sadly.

I suppose I was a bonnie laddie then, I was just turned sixteen, and I regretted I couldn't make my old friend happier. I told my father about it and he suggested I change the old man's dram from Johnny Walker to the Irish John Jameson. 'Give him that', he said, 'and he'll walk out singing, "The Wearin' of the Green." ' But I didn't bother, nor did I bother why my nationality should disturb the old man. I liked him and he liked me and that should have been enough.

I had to leave Craigneuk before I ever heard a child called a child; it was always a wean or a bairn. A pair of trousers were known as breeks, and 'Awa' an' bile your heid,' was a good-natured retort to most pleasantries. If they wished to state that a man was spending his time at home, the Craigneuk people would say, 'He's ben the hoose,' and the kindly advice not to worry over something usually came out as, 'Dinna fash yerself, laddie.'

Once my father settled back at work again I didn't fash myself for a long time. I was enjoying life even with my very limited income. To do so I had to have interests where money wasn't needed, and Hughie Clark my head barman helped me there. I acted second for him when he fought in the ring; I swung the towel between rounds while his brother Mick attended to his cuts and general condition. There weren't many cuts, else Hughie would have quit. It wasn't hard for us to get leave for his fights, they were midweek matches when the pub was quiet and they always took place in Bobby Dobbs' boxing booth. Dobbs was a coloured man of sixty at the time, but still pulled the gloves on, and was well known in the West of Scotland.

Hughie's brother was a rugged man who had fought professionally in America, and had taken some awful cloutings there, especially one from a famous fighter named Frank Klaus. But his brain was clear enough and he wore his crumpled ear and battered nose like badges of honour, which indeed was the way all Craigneuk sportsmen regarded them too. Hughie had other ideas; he carried his guard high, for he cherished his good looks.

Altogether I seconded him six times within a radius of six or seven miles, and he won each time on points. Dobbs paid him two pounds a time, which was real good money then for six two-minute rounds. Hughie always paid my car fare and gave me half-a-crown; he reckoned I brought him luck, not alone for winning, but that his handsome features got no permanent damage.

In return for my ring prowess he struggled hard to teach me how to waltz and how to reverse waltz. At that time proficiency in these dance movements meant a fellow would be welcomed by the girls in any dance hall in Scotland. I never got to do them really well, but I passed myself, just. I had no conversation while dancing; all my time was spent muttering one, two, three, one, two, three. I found the bands a bit of a nuisance: I felt I'd make a better waltzer with no music at all. Hughie presented me with a ticket for the very first ball I attended in Craigneuk. I went alone with no cab, no girl, no money, and had four waltzes with a nice little girl who was not long over from Donegal. We suited each other well, and ate sandwiches and drank minerals all on the house, and watched four drunken show-offs pummel away at each other. The girls screeched while the men fought, but Hughie, who could have beat all four with one hand, kept well away.

I saw my girl to her sister's door at six o'clock in the morning, wondering, but not asking how she risked attending the ball on her own. It just wasn't done in Craigneuk, not by the girls anyway; they liked to go by invitation with a gentleman and in a hired cab. It was only the real topnotchers who went home in a hired cab.

The ball was something of a turning point for me. I took

stock of myself with some pleasure and with more regrets. I had a huge mop of curly brown hair which I never combed, I just ran my fingers through it. I had very white teeth which I never brushed, there wasn't a toothbrush in our home. I needed a blue serge suit and a black silk knitted tie in the soft collar of a white silk shirt. A Hughie Clark garb, in fact: he was the dressiest young fellow in the 'Neuk', and I longed to be like him.

I put all this to my mother, more for a sympathetic understanding of my ambitions rather than any hopes of fulfilment from her. To my amazement she produced three pounds and told me to get on with it. I covered the lot for two pounds ten shillings and brought her the change back. It was a long time before I managed a ticket for another big dance, but I was well satisfied; I viewed myself with approval and I hoped one or two girls I knew were doing the same thing.

It was after that that I ceased my quick dive and sudden bankruptcy in the ice cream shops on the Saturday nights. I wanted all my money, four bob of it now, for bigger things. On my half-day off I donned my good blue serge with accessories, caught a train at Flemington station, and spent the time in Glasgow. It was a city that fascinated and horrified me. I had my father's habit of long lonely walks through the rough parts, the Gorbals, Cowcaddens, and Bridgeton Cross. The tenements seemed dirtier than in Craigneuk, the stairs steeper, the babies in their mother's shawls more fretful, and the men more cheerless as they left the public houses.

One early afternoon I passed a penny bazaar. There seemed to be no door on the premises, and on either side of a fairly wide passage were stalls with countless articles piled on them. There were few customers at the time and I paused at the entrance to glance at the articles on the nearest stall. As I did so a young girl moved swiftly past me to behind the stall, she was young, fourteen or so and likely not long left school. Where she was, was bad for colds and draughts; it was the position for the youngest employee. She looked as if she had hurried after lunch from a nearby tenement home and was without a coat. 'Has he come by yet, Mary?' she anxiously asked the nearest girl. 'Yes,' answered Mary happily, 'but he didna jaloose that you wisna here.' The girls saw me watching and listening and they smiled slightly, as if they knew that I shared their relief, which indeed I did. That was all, and I passed on thinking how that young girl would stand every day near to the pavement, and just for a few shillings weekly, and with the fear of dismissal if she was a few minutes late. It was all very puzzling, this clamp of poverty.

On each expedition I drank tea and ate meat pies and then off to a music hall, to Pickards Panopticon or to the Alhambra. Never once did I take a girl friend; I couldn't afford it, nor did I have a male friend. My job and its hours isolated me, but I was very happy in my loneliness.

One or two little incidents convinced me that I was a tall enough fellow and that my growing had all but ceased. The first was when I met Mr Moreiety on a Glasgow Street, I was almost a head taller than he was and I felt embarrassed for his sake. The second was seeing Peter Paxton coming into the 'Hive' and ordering a glass of whiskey and a pint of beer. Peter was a former classmate of mine at St Pat's, and he felt a lot more grown up than he looked. I couldn't see more than his head over the high bar, but he had been drinking plenty somewhere else. So much so that I hesitated to serve him, at which Peter protested loudly, and brought himself to the manager's attention. Little Geordie popped his head round his office door, took one look at Peter and said, 'Don't serve that bairn.'

So Peter was unlucky, but a day or so afterwards two more ex-classmates, Peter Scullion and Joey McNamara, stepped in and the boss himself served them without comment. Since drinking in a public bar was the first accolade to Craigneuk manhood, it looked as if childhood days were over.

My own attitude to drink didn't change. I had no religious scruples about it, I wasn't a teetotaller, I just didn't want it.

One day a man named Alick Slavin came in, looking quite prosperous too. He was a friend of my father and he was back on holiday from a steelworks in England. It was the new works of which my father had spoken many times lately, and all the more since his suspension. My father, who was working dayshifts that week, came in looking very warm, for he had just finished a charging up period. He was delighted to see Alick, the more so because he could now find out what a hot-metal, machine-charged, eight-hour-shift melting shop really meant to the furnacemen. It made him hopeful that such conditions would soon be enjoyed by all melters. He dearly longed for a whack himself and returned to his old problem, whether or no to relinquish his hard earned seniority and start at the bottom at the new place.

Besides, he had a great opinion of Englishmen from the days he had harvested in Cheshire. He considered them men of their word, with a straightforwardness his own race didn't possess. My father hated blarney and despised its practitioners. So at the beginning of 1914 he went down to Manchester to see for himself. If things were favourable he would seek employment, if not he would return home and forget it.

He came back, but only to clear up his affairs, and a fortnight later he began work in England. The day he started I gave my notice in at the 'Hive', for the home needed more than my fourteen shillings plus my brother's small wage. I would be seventeen the following September and I was quite big, and strong enough for a labouring post at my father's old place. The wages, nearly twenty-five shillings weekly, would be very useful until we joined him in England.

I was sorry to leave the pub, especially that first morning when I rose up just after five o'clock. It was cold and dark, and I hurried along thinking unhappily that at last I would see the other side of the main gates. Many a time I had wondered what lay beyond them. When I did pass through, there was nothing to see but bare ground. Away in the distance there were flames coming from raised edifices. Without knowing where I was going I walked along in a stream of silent, half-awake humanity. I'd been advised to ask for Mr Brown, the labourer's foreman, but no one seemed to know him.

The fourth man repeated the name until it rang a bell, 'Oh aye,' he said, 'you mean Sanny Broon the gaffer. You'll see him at the bottom of the melting shop steps, that's where his men line up for their jobs.'

He pointed to the furnaces away on the left. They were twenty-five feet or so above ground level, and beneath them, just where I stopped, it was known as the pitside. A welcome heat was rising from a still liquid pool that later I identified as slag. Altogether there were thirty of us awaiting Sanny Broon.

I knew it was him when he approached, for he wore the blue gutty collar of a foreman. It was his badge of office, the one thing most that separated him from the swine; otherwise he was as nondescript as the rest of us. He stood with a sheet of paper in his hand and assigned the workmen in small groups to various parts of the works. Most of them went first to a large shed and came out with varied equipment, heavy hammers, wedges, steel bars sharply pointed, shovels, and wooden wheelbarrows. He ascertained who I was, if I had a check number, and if the works' doctor had passed me fit the previous day. Then he sent me with four other men to empty a wagon of bricks on the melting shop.

The method of emptying was simple and regular. We propped up the door to make it a platform for the first man. He lifted two bricks clamped evenly together and swung them easily into the second man's hands. He swung them diagonally to the third man, who repeated the action to the fourth man. The fifth man stacked them neatly on the floor. I soon got used to it, and was glad that Sanny Broon had thoughtfully provided sacking to protect my hands.

I had always believed my boasting acquaintances who told me that no one ever was allowed to rest on the works. Now I pleasantly discovered that they were lying, for we had quite a few resting periods. Sanny Broon didn't seem to mind; each time he came he glanced at our progress and went off satisfied. I was so eager for my lunch when the hooter sounded midday that I was almost home before it ceased. I had a meal big enough for two men, and needed a lot of persuasion afterwards to go back and finish my day's work. My mother was horrified; she had never heard of a steelworker who reneged after lunch. Nor had I, but I was quite willing to be the first. We opened a second wagon of bricks and finished it before home time. I had more than enough, and my fingers were so crooked with the continual action that it was painful to straighten them.

The next day Sanny Broon ordered the whole gang to tear down the roof and linings of the B. furnace which was due for a general rebuild. Some, the wreckers, worked with hammers and steel wedges and bars. Others threw out the bricks they displaced, from the furnace bath. The rest of us filled them into wooden barrows and wheeled them away. The job lasted two weeks, and when it was still unfinished Sanny took me away to work in a chamber underneath the furnace. It had become clogged up with the wear and tear of many weeks of steelmaking. The function of this chamber was to trap the semi-liquid dust and debris that came with the waste gases as they left the furnace on the way to the chimney stack.

It was a dark solid substance and had cracked so much under prolonged water cooling that it wasn't hard to break up. We smashed the steel wedges underneath it, and levered it apart with the steel bars. It was warm work, and very enclosed, and we sweated freely. Lack of space compelled us to work in relays of three men each, the one group taking over while the other group rested.

Rather strange to say, I liked the job where many more dreaded it. I fancied myself with a fourteen-pound hammer, and took pleasure in crashing it with all my force on the steel wedge. It was very heartsome to see the slag break up with every clout I gave it. Later I found it could be heartbreaking when the wedges didn't budge despite my most determined efforts. I enjoyed the rest, too, as we sat with jackets thrown over damp shirts and drank sweet strong tea. It makes an overheated man feel even warmer but it is a pleasant and excellent strength reviver.

On Tuesday of my second week the B. furnace stood swept and free of all debris underneath and on top. It was ready for the bricklayers and their helpers, and I spent the rest of the week working on nightshift. My job was wheeling bricks to it, the ones we had unloaded on my first day. I was glad for six o'clock on Saturday morning; it gave me exactly a break of forty-eight hours.

The following morning I went to eleven o'clock mass at St Patrick's, and when it was over I stood in the crowd that thronged the roadway. The custom of standing that way was a throwback to the Sunday mornings in the Irish country-side. There people renewed friendships, crops were discussed, and likely enough the murders of English landlords were arranged. I know the Scots in Craigneuk considered us a great nuisance as they struggled past us with their bibles in their hands. They were great churchgoers at that time.

My mission was to report on steelworks life to Hughie Clark and Willie Ferris. They were very interested in the wages and conditions, 'Twenty-five bob a week', said Hughie, 'is no use to me. I get two pounds at the "Hive" and that's without swinging fourteen-pound hammers or shovelling tons of iron ore for it.'

'Or this,' I said, showing my work-scarred hands and broken nails. Hughie looked and shuddered, and glanced at his own well-groomed hands contentedly. 'My brother Mick', he said, 'is a contractor in the mines. He's offered me four pounds a week to go down coal-brushing.'

I shivered at the thought of the elegant Hughie working in a coal pit. 'I'm getting twenty-five bob a week in the "Hive"', said Willie, 'and I prefer it to a four-pounds-a-week job down a coal pit. A head barman's a somebody, but one doesn't know who the hell a miner is until he's washed.'

We all laughed and split up; Hughie to join his boxing mates in a gym over a stable: Willie to go off to a big pitch-and-toss school near the Craig coalpit, and I for an ice cream slider in the nearest Tally's shop.

8

The Art in Manual Labouring

There is more in labouring than just using a shovel, or in leaning on it. The labourer has an apprenticeship too, just as a prospective tradesman has one. In the labourer's case it is a private affair and there are no indentures. He gets no diplomas and he scarcely is aware of any skills, even when he has acquired them. The art is to bear the daily burden of tiredness and boredom equably, to know the limit of one's strength and to husband it. It is essential to know the right way to shovel, hammer, hold a wedge or a crowbar, carry loads, and to fill wheelbarrows. There is rhythm in these actions which protects the heart and lungs, and brings serenity to the mind. Without that rhythm the muscles shriek, the chest is strained, and the mind infested with frustration and anxiety.

Sometimes an old hand will put a young one right, but more often it comes with observation and lengthening ex-experience. It was Sanny Broon who showed me the way to use a long-shafted shovel. He showed me how to stand and how to dig the blade into the material, how much to lift, and how to swing it into, or from, a wagon. The tiresome way is to hold the shaft and haft rigidly from the beginning to end of each operation. The lightsome way is to let the shaft pass through the loosely clenched lower hand in the act of swinging.

The same operation is ideal in hammer swinging too. Grip one hand firmly at the shaft end and the other low down, and as the hammer rises let the lower hand slide up the shaft until it grips firmly just under the other hand to take its part in the crash down. If a load is too much for one's strength, well that's simple, let some one get on the other end. A strained back is a vicious thing and there are no prizes for weight-lifting or vanity. The most dangerous job and the simplest one was piglifting. It just had to be done the right way. Each long stick of iron weighed from one to two hundredweights; we labourers handled only the few that fell from the charge-wheeler's flat barrows. I watched the chargewheelers, the experts, before ever I attempted to lift one.

Each man upended the pig with two hands, the hands being protected by leathers, then steadied it on the floor vertically, and gently lowered the top end on the right thigh until the other end swung in balance. From that position they carried the pig away, rather in the fashion of one approaching with a battering ram.

The correct way to load a barrow is to spread the material evenly on the forepart and over the wheel, and not beyond one's strength. One little Irishman in the gang obeyed this rule so well that he wheeled half-loads of sand all one day to my full loads. It wasn't harming me any, but Sanny Broon noticed it and asked thoughtfully, 'Whit dae ye live on man?' The Irishman answered equally thoughtfully, 'Five-pence an hour,' and Sanny smiled faintly and moved off. Another Irishman went to extremes the opposite way, he proudly filled his barrow with heavy lump manganese so much that the shafts snapped clean in two when he lifted them up. Sanny Broon didn't like that.

The rest of us, myself included, made no public show of extra strength. Some seemed as old as the hills to me, but they all had a vitality which they could produce when occasion demanded, be it ever so reluctantly. Very likely it was poverty with all its stresses that made them seem so old, for I was no great judge of age at the time.

We all liked our sad, silent, little gaffer, it was the easiest thing in the world to do. I felt entirely at ease in his presence and that didn't happen to me with every one. I never heard him speak ill of any of us, but then he was almost too weary to talk at all. But there was more in him than just that, there was decency in him, he was observant, never once did he ask any one perform something beyond his strength. I was very grateful for his kindliness for I had heard alarming stories about the austerities of steelworks bosses. Yet no one had ever told me of Sanny Broon or, to give him his correct title, Alexander Brown. He never entered the Beehive in my time, nor did I ever see him go up or down the main street. I supposed he lived in the Motherwell direction, about a mile below Craigneuk.

A terribly cold snap came into the weather about the middle of February, and coal fires had to be sustained near all the important water pipes. It meant two men travelling round all parts of the works and carrying sacks of coal. A hot and cold job, and Sanny appointed Dinny Coyle and me for it first thing on the Monday morning. He looked at Dinny anxiously, and I knew why, for Dinny was white and shaken after Beehive whisky on the previous week-end. Worse than that was the rotgut stuff he drank in Lizzie Fullerton's shebeen. He was a week-end alcoholic who always made do with ether when the money ran out. That was dangerous stuff and could smother him if he didn't rift it up straight away. Dinny was a harmless civil fellow who was young and who would never live to be old. He was a neighbour of mine in Cowie's Square and had lived with us when his family became too riotous. His sister Sara was the best known prostitute in Craigneuk, and a right comely wreck she was too. She never reached a coat or a hat of her own, but always wore the long black shawl of the black Irish over her opulent figure. Her dark hair was curling and lovely and she died even younger than Dinny.

'Noo keep an eye on him,' muttered Sanny to me, 'he looks as if he's had a bucketful.' I nodded, and we both collected our sacks and filled them at the nearest coal wagon. The first fire was in a small brick cabin which had been built round the water pipes. We built it up and shovelled the ashes outside, and sat warming ourselves on two long forms.

There was a small roughly made table, when breakfast time arrived at half past seven. Dinny, who had hardly spoken, leaned his head on the table and went fast asleep. At that I rose up and determined to have one fast service at all the fires before breakfast. But the eight o'clock hooter was sounding the return to work before I got back. That didn't bother me for this was a lonely job where Sanny would never bother us. I read his mind plainly, he trusted me to do the work properly and to look after Dinny. I wakened Dinny and he drank some strong sweet tea but ate no food. He didn't look good.

After a leisurely breakfast I did my chores and returned to the cabin at half-past eleven. The fires would keep now until one-thirty. Dinny was still asleep and I wakened him to see how he was fixed for lunch. He didn't have any, nor did he intend to go home for any. I promised to bring him sandwiches back at one o'clock for there was no workmen's canteen. He nodded and went off to sleep again. After lunch I brought back a quart of tea in my deep-lidded can, and four good beef sandwiches. I wakened him up and he managed one sandwich but drank the tea almost to the bottom. I left him there still awake and went to my fires. It was nearly four o'clock when I returned and he was asleep again. He wakened up and finished the tea which I had placed near the fire. He ate no food but he had a little more conversation. It was mostly about how ill he felt and how he would be a changed man in future. I didn't answer, for I wasn't in the converting business, and I'd seen and heard a lot of Dinny's kind in Cowie's Square and in the Beehive. I gave him a shilling for a drink on the way home and went out at five for a last chore.

When I came back he had gone for the six o'clock hooter had sounded. The sandwiches were still on the table and I wrapped them up and put them in my pocket, for we didn't waste food in our home. My mother put the meat between two plates and said, 'We'll try Dinny boy with them to-morrow,' I answered doubtfully, 'If he turns out.' She laughed and said, 'He'll turn out. He's walking on the edge of a big high cliff but he won't fall over for a while yet.' My mother too had met Dinny's kind before.

The next morning the frost was still heavy and I made for the cabin without bothering to line up with the gang. Dinny was in the cabin before me and he was pounds better; he had brewed up, and was in good talking form. I produced the sandwiches and he ate them all to plenty of the tea, and then left with me to take his fair share of the work. At breakfast time he shared my sandwiches, and went home for his lunch when the midday hooter sounded. He refused a shilling from me at the end of the day and that didn't surprise me, for normally he wasn't a sponger.

The rest of the week went by uneventfully. The terrible cold persisted and we played no football at the week-end. On the Monday morning I went back to the fires to meet a Dinny in the identical state of the previous Monday. 'I'll leave him to you again,' muttered Sanny when he called in the cabin. I nodded, and went off to do the chores alone. All the time, no management took any notice of us, or looked inside the cabin. Yet it was a very strict place and Dinny would have been sacked on the spot, and maybe Sanny too for his kindliness. On the Tuesday morning Dinny was once more a good workman, and remained that way till the thaw split our partnership at the following week-end. He looked in good trim when we lined up for fresh jobs on the Monday morning. It was just as well, for Sanny sent him to cut the slag out of the chamber of the A. furnace. He would never have assigned that to a sick Dinny.

When I got home for lunch there was a letter from my father. It was brief, for letter writing was a major agony to him, but the news was good. He liked his job, and the district, and the English way of life. He hoped soon to have a home for us. It put new heart in my mother who spent most of her time wondering how he was. My brother Peter was mildly interested; he was fifteen and always galloped off happily to his rolling mill job. My sister Anna Mary was still a schoolgirl at St Patrick's and looked forward to living in England. She had never met an Englishman in her life. I had met but two, they were Charlie and Willie Woods who came from Chorley to live with their aunt in Craigneuk.

The slag in the A. furnace pockets proved a far harder task than Sanny anticipated. So a fresh gang, myself included, was sent along to work nightshifts on it. There were six of us and as usual we worked in groups of three, and this time we had to fight for every shovelful. There was no smoothness at all in it, and the wedges became blunted with our efforts. Each night we started at six o'clock and worked steadily to first supper at nine. There was an hour break which I spent at home, and would gladly have stayed there. At ten we resumed and worked steadily through till second supper at one in the morning. This was a long affair till two-thirty and really was the boundary of our intense effort. From then on we took it easy, the deadly tiredness of nightshift was upon us, and we had bought our ease by our earlier efforts.

We had no direct boss over us, Sanny of course remaining on days, but each morning he could see at a glance how we laboured.

During the long break I used to go on the melting shop to talk to any furnacemen I knew. Some of them I knew as Beehive patrons, and some were neighbours from Cowie's Square. The melting shop was known as the 'New Side' to distinguish it from the older melting shop which lay just across from it. The New Side contained basic open hearth furnaces and the Old Side contained acid open hearth furnaces. My father had worked on the New Side and it was gratifying that so many of his former workmates inquired about him.

One of them was a powerfully built Irish chargewheeler, very strong, and very awkward with great splay feet. His temper was just as awkward and I used to dread serving him in the 'Hive'. This night he inquired civilly enough about my father. I answered the same way and was rather surprised at his forbearance. The next second he was true to form for he hissed, 'He's twice the man you are.' I was quite willing to agree to such a claim at any other time and be happy about it. But the sight of the venom dripping from his puss enraged me, and I answered, 'Yes and he's ten times a better man than you are, you big ugly bastard.' There was a great satisfaction in rolling the last word round my tongue, and I was prepared to pay for my pleasure, for he was very strong. To my surprise he didn't move or speak. He just stood looking at me in astonishment with his mouth open. I resisted the temptation to grind my heavy boots in his big flat feet, and walked off instead. When I looked back he was still in the same position, with his mouth still open like a gap in a hedge. I saw him many times afterwards but he never came near me again.

I had different treatment altogether a few moments afterwards from a first-hand melter named Jock Steenson, and up to them a complete stranger to me. I'd helped him raise the middle door of his furnace; they could be very awkward when the balancing weight slipped. In a return of civility he handed me his blue spectacles and invited me to gaze at the white-hot mass inside. It was the first time I ever did it.

He said, 'That's not metal you're looking at, it's slag, the metal is underneath it. It's my job to open the slag with iron ore and get the whole lot boiling. That way the metal will bubble its impurities into the slag.' He signed to two other melters and all three of them lashed in iron ore from a heap on the floor. The sweat poured from them long before they quit. As I moved on I hoped to see the result of their labours before I left the melting shop.

The next man I saw was a first-hand named Paddy O'Hare. He was a friend of my father, and being short, stout, and fifty, he was always named, 'Paddy the Hare.' That night he was a busy man as he directed the charging of his furnace. Standing before the open furnace doors the melters shovelled in piles of light steel scrap and followed that up with pigiron, with which they lined the bath. Each man, four in all, slid a stick of iron from a neat stack and walked leisurely forward. In turn they placed each stick on a long flat-ended iron rod known as a 'peel'. Immediately the man holding the peel moved it swiftly inside the furnace, and neatly turned the iron on top of the previous one.

I didn't wait, but I knew that the next job would be shovelling lime and iron ore into the bath. The operation was lengthy and exhausting, and resting between whiles was necessary. This caused no delay, for the flame would be still doing its work in melting down the materials. The last part would see the heaviest steel scrap being manoeuvered in by the peel. That completed the operation, and unless there were furnaces to tap out, the melters rested or went about lighter jobs. It would take four or five hours before the charge melted into liquid and was ready for the refining stage.

As I walked back Jock Steenson called me over to see the results of the iron ore feed. The door was raised and he handed me the blue spectacles, 'Gimme your opinion,' he said smiling. I smiled too at the thought; nevertheless I noticed that the liquid inside was bubbling from end to end. 'It's doing its work,' the melter said, 'it's transferring the phosphorus and the carbon and other elements from the metal to the slag. The boil, laddie, is the important thing on steel furnaces.'

Before I left I asked him what steel was. I had a fair idea, but I lacked a definition if any one chanced to ask me. He was surprised. He'd never been asked that before, he had never asked himself that. He thought a while and then said, 'Well there's no doubt it's a tough metal, but not a pure one, for mankind has a lot to do with it. We take the iron, which is a fine metal in itself, and we refine it by great heat. Then we add alloys, manganese and the like, to make it stronger still.' He thought a while longer, then said, 'No, I can't improve on that. But thanks for asking.' 'Thanks for telling me,' I naturally replied, and with good reason. Just because he was interested in his job he had made me interested too. It gave me a glimmer that steelmaking contained more than exhausting labour for the melters. There was the satisfaction of creation in every pot of good steel. That made up for a lot.

It was on Paddy the Hare's furnace that I first saw a break-away. It happened just beneath the sillplate on the middle door, and I rather thrilled at the very spectacular sight. I sympathised too with the poor fellows who had to clear it all away, the more so when I found out that I was one of them. It was the rule that Sanny Broon's gang should be called in to such emergencies.

When the metal ceased flowing we hosed it straight away until it was black. Then we hammered steel wedges under the ragged mass which might have weighed fifteen tons. Once the wedges had lifted it a trifle we inserted steel crowbars to raise some more. Then we slung steel ropes round it and a steam crane tugged it away in large ragged pieces. All the time the stifling atmosphere was filled with the steam of dirty water, bad tasting stuff it was too. We had to stand often on the metal to tug the steel ropes tight, and that burned our feet as well as our boots. It was a three hours job before we put sweeping brushes on it. 'I suppose it all makes variety,' said Paddy the Hare unhappily as he handed me a lidful of tea. I didn't want such variety but there was truth in his words. In the face of such hazards, it made the creation of good steel more satisfying still.

I was glad to get home for lunch that day and to change into dry clothes. Not all Sanny's gang went home at lunch-time and they would be wet and uncomfortable for the rest of the day. The melters were different, for they were equipped for torrid conditions. Their flannel shirts absorbed the sweat, while retaining their heat, and the sweat towels were a god-send. Their heavy sailcloth aprons protected their legs from the heat, and that was their job any way, experts in heat. Out in the open digging holes in ground might have given them pneumonia, but inside a melting shop they were the nearest thing to firebricks.

In July a letter from my father said that he expected to rent a house in a very short time, and that jobs were plentiful for Peter and me. I hoped that meant the melting shop for me and I was glad that we were leaving Scotland. I saw little future there on the hand-charging furnaces. I doubted whether my strength would ever face up to them, for not one in every five men could stand up to the punishment. I began to take longer looks at the Craigneuk streets as I walked along them. Black though they were I knew I would miss them, and the Wishaw Pavilion and the Craigneuk Music Hall. I used always to attend one or the other of the two halls every week, and always with a mate or two from the football team. I never took a girl with me for I never had the money; actually I depended on free passes from the Beehive. It was the same with the Saturday evening dances at the Hibernian Hall. It only cost a shilling but I made sure that I only paid for myself. I could do no other on four and six-pence pocket money. The girls I danced with never got much conversation for I still had to concentrate on the old one, two, three.

When Willie Ferris gave notice to quit the pub that looked the end of my free passes, but before the end of the week little Geordie doubled his wages to two pounds ten shillings weekly. Without asking Hughie Clark had his wage doubled to four pounds weekly. They were astounded, but the first world war was imminent and Geordie wanted to hold them as long as he could.

I hadn't been reading the newspapers myself, it was a habit that would grow later, and the coming conflict wasn't much in my mind. When it did break out I was astounded at the change in men. So far as I know all my classmates at St Patrick's joined up in the first few weeks. They were all keen on the kiltie regiments, the Gordons, and Camerons, and the Black Watch. I didn't go with them; I liked the swing of the kilts as well as any of them, but I lacked their gay generosity and their spirit. The war I felt would have to wait awhile, I was under age, and I wished to see my family settled.

I was seventeen a month after the war started and we were still in Craigneuk, still waiting the call to England. When it came we didn't take long to pack; we could have put our valuables in a matchbox. My mother had only gladness that we would be joining my father again, but still she felt it, as she looked round our one room home. She had made it a real home, for once behind our door with its shining nameplate, we had always felt as safe as the king in his castle. Now it was nearly all over I began to count the hours, begrudging each one passing. Craigneuk had become very precious to me.

I quit my job a week before we left, for I had much to do and friends to say goodbye to. I made sure to shake hands with Sanny Broon and tell him how much I appreciated working under him. He was very nice about it in his sad way. There was warmth in his handshake and sincerity in his 'You're all right laddie, I liked you fine. Good luck.'

I went into the Beehive the night before we left. I wanted to say goodbye over a glass of whisky; it would be the first I ever ordered in the 'Hive', or anywhere else. To my disappointment every one was missing save a new lad in my place, a real Craigneuk cockie. There were only two customers in the bar, and I enquired about Willie and Hughie. 'They've gone,' he said briskly, 'I'm the boss now. Want to leave a message?' 'No', I answered, 'I'll come back when there's men around.'

The next morning I said goodbye to Willie and Hughie and never thought about drinking at all. Little Geordie wasn't there. We went to Flemington Station, high above the road and right against the steelworks. I could see the pug engines huffing up and down, and hear the chug chug of the powerhouses. All my life in Craigneuk, night and day, they were my most familiar sounds. They were the last ones I heard as the train left the station.

D

9

England

What my father promised, he fulfilled. We could hardly believe it but our home had three bedrooms, kitchen, living room, bathroom, hot and cold water, and electric light. The water closet was outside, but for our use only and not shared by eight families. The surroundings were not pretty, for the terrace we lived in stopped short at the steel works' rear entrance. Just beyond that entrance was a slag tip and a slag crushing department. I didn't mind such trifles, I had always lived near a steelworks gate, but this one provided spectacles. It gave fireworks displays that cost me nothing.

In Craigneuk there were no blast furnaces producing iron; the steel works had to buy it from outside. Here there were blast furnaces tapping metal by day and night, and tipping the slag within sight of our door. The rush of the locomotive with its ladle of white hot liquid was always a thrill. It stopped for nothing and the steam whistle shrilled all the way. It used to waken me in the night time and I would wait for the silence at the end of the run. Then the engine would gently push up the bogie between it and the ladle, while the shunter adjusted the chains. Then one fierce clashing, tightening move and over would go the blazing stream like a sudden dawn.

When it did I always glanced at the alarm clock, then waited for the darkness to come into its own again. Then I'd fall asleep with no trouble at all.

My father had scrubbed much before we arrived and there was plenty more to do. We all worked hard to make it look good, for we were proud of it and glad of the chance. It was

84

the first time I ever helped paper a wall; up to then we had very little wall to paper. I would have dug the garden too, it was something I looked forward to, but there was none to dig. 'It will come,' said my father, 'there are plenty of houses with gardens in this place, only I took the first chance available. We will move out when we see something better.'

We did too, eventually, and he had his garden and a fowl run, and enough outhouses to make it look like real estate. He had settled down to his chargewheeling job and would never become a first-hand melter again. There wasn't the time left, he was forty-seven, the same age as my mother, and given normal promotion it would take twenty-five years to reach the top again.

My brother Peter was the first, as usual, to go out and find work. He became a driver of an electric grab crane, a high overhead affair that filled the bunkers of the gas producers with coal. I had a look at the district before I went near the steel works. It was no great shakes but better looking than the 'Neuk', and the inhabitants served many other trades besides steelmaking. This helped, for districts entirely given over to the heavy industries are very depressing to gaze on. That's if one knows anything better, which I didn't.

The main street was a part of the road that ran from Manchester to Liverpool. It was very busy with steam lorries puffing along with great loads of raw cotton and finished cloth. The lorries seemed very unreliable, and disconsolate drivers and mates patching them up became a very familiar sight to me. The steelworks and its offices lay just behind the main road, and right down to the bank of the Ship Canal. That was interesting, for ships are always interesting, and I used to watch them being coaled not far from our street. The seamen, very often coloured, passed our front door frequently. So much so that our quarter was known as 'Alabama' by the whole district. They seldom got further than the pub at the end of the street.

There were far more steelworkers going and coming on the main road than in the 'Neuk'. It was a bigger works for one thing, and the eight-hour shift system on the producing end set men moving three times in every twenty-four hours, as compared to the twice daily movement of the twelve-hour shifts in Craigneuk.

I easily recognised the melters among them, for their style was very similar to the Scottish ones. Many of them walked off heated, sometimes sweat-drenched, with the same in-difference to health, their jackets not buttoned over their flannel shirts, and their sweat towels tucked in their broad belts and trailing the ground. I followed one of them, a very fine looking man who I knew later on as Billy Gale, into a pub named the 'George and Dragon'. I was curious to see the nature and size of his drink after his shift on the furnaces. He drank one pint of beer, and out. I was astounded. There certainly was a difference between this class of steelman and the sort I'd known.

The pubs were different too, if the 'George' was anything to go by. It was a neat affair where sawdust would have been out of place, and barmaids were serving in the small two-sided bar. It was my first sight of barmaids, for I came from where it was men only behind the bars, and the bigger the better. All up and down the steel towns of the West of Scotland, the barmen were chosen for size as carefully as the policemen were. I was five-foot-ten myself when I entered the 'Hive', and even though I daren't say 'Bo' to a goose, there were lots of the awkward customers too cock-eyed to realise it.

Instead of a stand-up drinking den the 'George & Dragon' offered plenty of pleasant rooms with much comfortable seat-ing accommodation. The thought struck me that here were places where a man could take his wife or his girl and not be ashamed or apprehensive. I liked the English pubs from that moment, and I was only too willing for them to civilise me to their way of life.

I had no trouble at all in landing a job on the melting shop, but not as a chargewheeler on the furnaces; that came later. I had first to go labouring, emptying wagons of anthracite coal, wheeling it near a furnace to dry, and then filling it into large paper bags. The third-hand melters wheeled them away to be used in the steelmaking. My wages were 27s. 6d. weekly, and I started and quit at eight to five each day. Saturday was a half-day finish at one and Sunday was free.

I spent six weeks on this job and since it was easy I had plenty of time to look around me. Here everything for steelmaking was gathered together in a complete unit. From the coke ovens came the fuel to burn the iron from the ore, in the blast furnaces. It went from there, still liquid, to the steel furnaces. From there as steel it was teemed in the moulds, solidified into ingots, re-heated in the soaking pits, crunched through the cogging mill, drawn out in the big mill, cut by the saws, and sent off to the munition makers to become shells for the guns.

I thought a modern steel works like this would be better in every way than the old one I'd left. I was wrong. The canny Scottish steelmasters with years of experience behind them didn't waste a thing. The new place, with a war on top of it almost as soon as it started, wasted plenty. The time check system was bad. Each morning I picked up a timesheet and filled it in at the end of my day, my name, number, department, rate, and the hours worked. The melting shop manager signed it and I dropped it in a box for the purpose on the way out.

That seemed simple enough, but there were never any wages for me at the pay office. I had always to fight for an emergency pay note each week. The cashier never failed to tell me sourly that I was a thief who just filled in a timesheet and claimed wages on the strength of it. He suspected many were doing just that, and I found out later that it was so. A while afterwards he lost his job in a hurry, and two of his staff were jailed.

I was glad when I went chargewheeling for I needed no timesheet then. The stocktaker on each shift acted as timekeeper too. The fellow on my shift was very liberal, he marked every one present when they were absent, and shared the spoils. He was caught in the end and prosecuted along with one of his accomplices.

It was a time of coming and going, a restless time, men were quitting and joining the forces, and the forces were dumping them back to their jobs. Some of them wore regimentals when their working shift was over each day. They seemed loth to part with them at the end of the war. Three of them, all furnacemen, had been sent back from Highland Regiments. They simply loved the kilts. Not even Tommy McKinnon, a sarcastic old first-hand from Scotland, could dent their pride. Each time he met them he took his pipe from his mouth, spat carefully, and inquired mildly, 'Nae bagpipes?'

One time I was walking down Oxford Street in Manchester when three smashing looking Highlanders came swiftly down in the opposite direction. They were arm in arm, arrogantly forcing people off the pavement, gay as larks, and gloriously fit. 'Home on leave,' I heard one lady say as she turned to admire them. But they weren't, they were my three furnace colleagues, out on a bender.

At seventeen-and-a-half I found I could manage the chargewheeling all right. There were two of us on each furnace and the jobs were various. We filled long metal boxes from wagons of lime, iron ore, iron scalings, steel scrap, and sometimes pigiron. These boxes tipped the material into the furnaces during the process of charging up, and at other times, according to the first-hand melters' judgment. The boxes were the product of the firm's huge moulding shop, and were shaped so that the charging machine rams slotted in easily and safely. Once gripped, the load swung round to the furnace door with the driver at his controls guiding it in. It was the work of moments to turn the box, empty, withdraw, swing round, release the empty on the filling bench opposite the furnace, pick up the next full box, and repeat the operation again and again.

The machines were exceedingly mobile, electric of course, and the drivers could rattle up and down the melting shop on

multifarious errands at a height of six inches to six feet from
the floor. The furnaces were all fifty tons capacity basic open
hearth type, and given a straight run with good steel scrap,
could be charged in three hours or less. The machines were
very noisy but so expert were the drivers in charging up, that
the sounds became rhythmic.

The whole shop was a conglomeration of ear-splitting
noises. Besides the charging machines there were the seventy-
tons-capacity cranes operating high over the pit side, adjacent to the melting shop. They crashed and bashed and
grinded and clanged like all hell let loose. Their most important job was to clamp their huge arms in the sockets of the
ladles at tapping times on the furnaces, then convey their
white-hot sparkling loads to the casting cranes. The casting
cranes from where the steel was teemed into the moulds were
downright death traps. They became obsolete when men
were seriously burned and even died of their injuries.

There would have been little danger if steelmaking con-
formed to set rules and regulations, but it didn't then, and
it's doubtful if it ever will.

It was a sight to terrify the bravest teemer or pitman, as he
stood on that rickety casting crane, and watched a ladleful of
wild metal bearing down on him, with its gases lashing it over
the side. It would not be the sort of steel the furnaceman intended, but it sometimes happened that way despite him.

Another noise, and a frequent one, came from locomotives
and their continual shunting on the rail track that ran
parallel to the melting shop. The shunter's whistle, allied to
the engine whistle, and the staccato crashing of wagon buffers
in a long line, were all splendid warnings for one to keep the
wits moving as well.

The second biggest job for chargewheelers was wheeling
dolomite from the crushing mill to the furnace floor. It had to
be ready there for the bath repairers whenever the furnace
had tapped its charge. Sometimes these repairs were of short
duration, sometimes they lasted many hours, so that the
dolomite was continually applied. It was a mineral, a mix-

ture of lime and magnesite, that had to be quarried, dried, burned, and moderately crushed before reaching the melting shop.

The furnace baths were composed of this material and when shovelled into the holes and crevices left by the charge, it became part of the bath proper. But it was only successful when applied in a very high furnace temperature. This made 'fettling' as it was called, a very warm and uncomfortable affair. It was a split-second action; one went to the open furnace door with a loaded shovelful, took lightning aim, swung, and retreated. Even a second's delay could cause active burning to the body.

Another chargewheeler's job was wheeling fluorspar to the furnaces. This was a heavy yellow material, not unlike some iron ore. Its purpose was to thin thick slags in the furnaces and make them available for more lime. Melters did this when eliminating high sulphurs in the metal. Strictly, the chargewheelers provided the material and left the rest to the melters, but it seldom worked out that way. We dived into the fettling to give the sweating melters a lift, and the same with the charge feeding, we lashed in the iron ore with the rest. At tapping times too we crashed the bar through the tapholes with the heavy hammers, and staggered back as the metal flowed. When the samplepasser whistled a signal we shovelled the manganese into the stream. No one paid us extra money for it, though the grateful melters might tip a bob or two at the weekends.

We were preparing for the day when we would take our first third-hand shifts, and they could be hectic if we hadn't the knowhow.

Besides all this, the chargewheelers were the tea brewers and the beer carriers.

Like most things, there was luck in chargewheeling, good or bad. We always examined the steel scrap wagons with interest, and the weather, for where we unloaded there was no roof. Sometimes it would be handy stuff, like neat heavy billet ends from our rolling mill. We'd empty, just the two of us, two ten-ton loads in good style. Sometimes it would be tangled turnings from engineering places, and that could be the devil. Sometimes it was a novelty, like a wagon load of shoehorns, or a terrible tangled load of rusty steel needles. The last were the worst of all, for it needed pickaxes to free each shovelful, and just one fugitive needle had the blade bouncing off its objective.

The scrap stock pile, which covered thousands of tons, was treasure trove to the handy men. Bicycle wheels and frames, lawn mowers and motor jacks, everything that was metal came along in time. The department was contracted and the head of it was a reasonable man. With a signed note to the works police one could take off what could be carried.

But the pile went, when the scrap steel became very scarce at a later part of the war. We were as short of it as any one else, and not much better off from the stuff that the scrap drive yielded. That was a government affair, and we got very little good metal from the countless gates and railings that came along.

I had one unfortunate adventure in the scrap drive. I'd taken a short cut in thick fog through a public park. When I reached the big ornamental gates I found them padlocked for the very first time. I climed over and tore my trousers badly. A few days afterwards I stood looking at the still locked gates very thoughtfully. They stood alone; the local council had dedicated the surrounding railings to the scrap drive, but preserved the gates.

What pleased me most about chargewheeling was my ability to stand up to it. I was good with a hammer and good with a shovel, and I felt that I had learned a trade. There was nothing wonderful about the wages, at least I can't remember any exhilaration on my part. We had a shift-working system at the time which allowed six shifts on the early morning turn from six o'clock until two. On the afternoon our working week was five shifts, and on the nightshift we started at two o'clock on the Sunday afternoon and worked straight through sixteen hours to six o'clock Monday morning. From there we worked eight-hour shifts until the following Saturday morning. That made it a fifty-six-hour week, with the discomfort of a dreary double shift to start it, and the monotony of nightwork thrown in. The first time I did it in 1915 I thought it was worth more than the £2. 8s. 5d. marked on my pay packet. Still, it was a bit of an occasion, for up to then it was the highest wage I had ever earned.

10

On the Furnaces

My first regular chargewheeling job was on the G. furnace under a man named Billy Lane. He was very young to be a first-hand steel melter, only twenty-six years old. He wasn't the only young leading hand, for the works, being only established three years, had provided a fine opportunity for ambitious steelmen.

'Are you new here?' he asked me as I made to hang my jacket up in the small portable wooden cabin. 'Yes,' I answered nervously, for I felt ill at ease with these confident English melters, their accents bothered me too. 'Are you in the melters' union?' he went on. I wasn't in any trade union, but being the son of my father I intended to join one quickly.

At Billy Lane's directions I went to the mixer furnace, a few yards away, and inquired for Billy Edwards the man in charge of it. He was also the branch secretary of the Iron & Steel Trades Federation. Later on it became a Confederation and more popularly known as BISAKTA. Edwards, a middleaged Welshman, soon directed me how to join the trade union. The two men sitting beside him, Billy Hodge, his second-hand, and the third-hand George Dennison, were both from good trade union stock. Billy's uncle being John Hodge the founder of the British Steel Melters Union and George's brother becoming its general secretary.

The mixer furnace they worked on didn't produce like the other furnaces, but was a repository in which the liquid iron from the blast furnaces was partially refined before going on to the steel producing ones. It was a tilter, and its huge mass

93

could move forwards and backwards as silently and as easily as shutting or opening a door.

My promptness in joining our trade union, allied to my quick return to get busy on the furnace, seemed to impress Billy Lane for he was very pleasant to me. I thanked heaven he was easy, for some of the first-hands wasted little time in being civil to chargewheelers. There was a tradition about their lofty standing in the steel trade. These fellows from the other steel towns in Britain had brought it with them to this new works. Most likely they had suffered the arrogance of superiors at some time, and now reckoned that it was their turn.

Tradition has often retarded progress in the British steel trade, but I like a trade with some tradition nevertheless. It helps a man feel less of a parvenu. In Billy Lane I found an enthusiast; he was proud of his job, his trade, and his skill. Without dreaming he did so he helped to make the life a lot more interesting to me.

Soon after I started on the G. furnaces the government whipped the trade into a far more collective effort. The cohesion didn't mean much to me at the time but it gave Lane satisfaction. He reckoned we had made our first real step towards winning the war.

The melting shop manager, a man named Barker, was a relative of Lane, and I thought that was the base of his skill. It gave him confidence to handle his furnace and to experiment in his steelmaking. Where other first-hand melters dare not step out of line lest their theory be wrong. Lane was often doing the unorthodox and getting away with it three times out of four. Billy loved to see the steel come quietly to perfection in its stocking feet. Which was a melter's way of saying that the steel had been made quickly, quietly, without excessive labour, or expense. That sort of steel melting was good for the firm, good for the men, and happened fairly often to the more skilled melters. To some of the first-hands it never happened, even when the furnace and the charge inside it was co-operative, and it could be at times; even then they were blind to it when steel was being offered to them on a plate. Instead of sitting down and lighting a pipe or eating a sandwich, they had to be up loud-mouthed and about, knocking hell out of the metal and the life out of their unfortunate underlings. In the end they always made steel but there was little tiptoeing in stocking feet about it, rather it seemed to limp ruefully from the furnace.

In my youthful ignorance I started off by regarding these nincompoops as little steel gods, but I soon became astonished at their incompetence. I suppose it couldn't have happened in peacetime in an old-established works. There was one first-hand I only knew as the 'Stone Doddler' who could be almost guaranteed to stone doddle any furnace he took over. One afternoon our samplepasser, a lazy old boy named Freddy Hall, relieved his mate as usual a half hour before the rest of us came on. The Doddler's furnace was in grand condition, the charge inside of it was ready for tapping, with a good slag, good temperature, and boiling in lovely fashion. Freddy congratulated the Doddler's mate and went on first of all to see the condition of all the other furnaces. When he came back the Doddler had taken over, and had slammed a box of iron ore into the furnace, reduced the flame and so ruined the temperature as well as the chemical analysis. It was eight o'clock in the evening, a six hours' delay, before we tapped the charge. 'The bloody man', groaned Freddy, meaning the Doddler, 'should be making ice cream.'

Billy Lane lived two railway stations away in a place named Urmston, and sometimes he overslept on the early morning turn. When that happened his place was filled by the senior second-hand whose name was Hayton. Hunky Dory Hayton was the title he usually got. Hunky's performances were often a lesson to me; they showed the difference between a skilled confident steelmaker and a willing nervous one.

One morning he took over it seemed as if all the luck was against him. The furnace stood there sinister, threatening, overcharged, overheated, and sizzling with carbon. Hunky's task was to reduce the carbon and also to get the sulphur and phosphorus well out of the metal. His immediate concern, though, was to keep the charge inside the furnace, and it looked a tricky proposition.

He started off by bitterly condemning the first-hand he had relieved, for neglecting his job and allowing the temperature to become excessive. That was little use, the man would likely be asleep in bed at the time, but it was traditional in steelmaking to blame the 'other shift' for everything. As Hunky spoke the white hot slag rose high up in the furnace and flowed from all the doors on to the floor. He dived to the reversing gear, threw the gas and the air levers over hurriedly, and caused the flame to disappear entirely for a second or so. Before it could blaze in at the other end, the furnace met its Waterloo, and so did Hunky. The slag, with no flame to hold it down, rose up in a fearsome white mass, pouring out with six times its previous volume, and whipped out the whole of the front lining. We barely managed to rescue our clothes from the burning portable cabin.

The sight of the blazing wreck, for which he was in no way responsible, nearly set the poor fellow crazy. Fortunately at that moment his cool collected second-hand, Tommy Marsh, appeared and took over. He lengthened the flame by reducing the air, and when the slag subsided he had the charging machine drop in two boxes of lime. Then he sent for the fettling bricklayers, the emergency men, and he didn't need to tell them what to do.

It was a devil of a makeshift job, for they had to steady each silica brick on a hand peel, and build it against the furnace buckstays. Their bodies were partially protected by hastily thrown up corrugated iron sheets, which burned quickly and needed replacing. Their hands were protected with pieces of sacks, and when they were exhausted others took their places.

To help them Hunky reduced the temperature as much as he dared, for he had to keep the charge in liquid. All the time the men worked standing on corrugated sheets thrown over the barely solid slag. Their boots and clogs burned, their feet almost roasted, but they finished the job and the lining held.

The melters, all three of them, myself, and my charge-wheeler mate who was young and Irish, and named Micky McDermott, then got down to the slag clearing job. In between whiles Hunky's fortune had risen, for the metal sample he forwarded to the laboratory showed the way clear for tapping save twenty points of carbon. 'We can boil that out while we have a sandwich,' said he. It was eleven o'clock and he had yet to break his fast. The rest of us had not been so self sacrificing.

We had her running down the lander as the twelve o'clock hooter sounded. We spent the next hour repairing the damage with dolomite. Then Hunky handed over to the fettling bricklayers, to get down to the job of building a more lasting, but still emergency lining, and with no flame to scorch them.

It was home time for the furnace crew and we left the bricklayers at it, as we greeted our relieving mates. Hunky hadn't done so badly at all. He had made good steel in the face of great difficulties, and he had preserved his sanity. He ordered five pints, one for each of us, in the Railway Inn, and he did it twice. Each time we raised the full measures to his health and prosperity, Tom Marsh the second-hand, Harry Greenman the third-hand, Micky McDermott and me. 'I'll tell yo what lads,' said Hunky, 'Billy Lane couldn't have done one damn bit better.'

We all sincerely and truthfully agreed. It was the very highest praise.

If there was any privations during that first war, for myself I mean, well I can't remember them. I was very often hungry, but it didn't need a war to cause that, not with my kind of an appetite. If there were privations, I'm sure now that they were good for me. I know that the rationing system in the second world war was a tremendously good and healthful thing. So I've no reason for thinking that the first one did me harm. Besides I didn't want anything extra, there was lots of scorn for war profiteers, and it was nice not being one of them.

I was a few-pounds-a-week man in a vital trade, and that was the way I wanted it. Even at that it wasn't too easy being a civilian in that first war. Old ladies with fearful bumps of righteousness were handing out white feathers to civilians who looked military age. They were constantly having to apologise to soldiers in mufti, and to others for their hasty patriotism. They never approached me, for which I thanked heaven, but I was always in dread of them and not even my arm band comforted me.

The khaki armlet was a government issue proving that one had been attested for military service but was engaged on vital munition work. I hated mine and never wore it, for I felt it was a poor substitute for a Gordon Highlander's kilt. That was my secret gnawing if only my cravenness had stepped out of line a little. I would not have been a brave soldier, I'd have been an eternally frightened one, but knowing myself better later on, I feel sure I would have plodded along and taken whatever came my way. Just as so many very unprofessional soldiers did. When the war finished men who had not been in the forces, unless they were sincere pacifists, could feel as if they had been blackballed from a great warmhearted courageous company. There were many times in the presence of men at work, or in company, when I had to be silent. When they talked of service days there was nothing for me to say.

In those days there were times too when silence was a good thing. After the Irish Rising in 1916 the police used to send spies among us. We Irish, and there were plenty of us, had no special pub to meet in. We used to stand at the corner of St Teresa's Catholic Church near to the steelworks, and our subjects would be innocent enough but the police didn't think so. The spies they sent were the most decrepit Irishmen we had ever seen. They were never young, always down at heel, and most likely released only recently from jails. We could spot them a mile away and quit talking immediately they thrust their unsavory persons upon us. We despised the authorities too for such stupid clumsiness.

St Teresa's was a rather small church which had been donated by the great Lancashire Catholic family of De Traffords. The congregation was about evenly divided between English and Irish, and the two groups disliked each other. The English took an interest in their religion and could answer questions on it. The Irish mostly stood at the back fingering rosaries instead of missals and were vague about the fundamentals of their faith.

I was in that group and used to stand at the back even when there were unoccupied seats all around me. Yet I was as firm a Catholic as the English portion and so were the other Irishmen. We all believed it a mortal sin to miss mass on Sundays and we tottered out no matter how drunk we had been the night before. All those men like myself were impregnated with Catholicity from the time they could look up and take notice. It didn't do them any harm; in fact the chief characteristic I noted in them, and myself, was a great harmlessness.

We used our religion like a comfortable blanket, and we peeped out in cowardly fashion, but with complacency, at a world of atheists and agnostics. For myself it helped to make most of my virtues negative ones; I didn't commit adultery and I didn't covet my neighbour's wife. There were a whole host of minor didn'ts, but those were the main two. I was particularly anxious to avoid committing the main two, for whatever the immediate pleasure I knew with my upbringing that my retrospects would be tortuous, and I like my retrospects to be tidy. Now that I'm old I enjoy the tidyness and still say that so far as I'm concerned the Catholic Church is a fine institution and that I'm very happy to be a member of it.

Once I got the hang of the melting shop and could better understand the accents of the Yorkshire and the North Eastern melters, I was content enough. I was nineteen years old in the September of 1916 and appropriately I got my first promotion on my birthday. It was an early morning turn and an unusual number of melters hadn't turned out. I was very excited about it although the move to third-hand melter was for one day only.

The work was varied and most of it strenuous. I had to wheel various alloys used in steelmaking to the furnace. Some of it, the heaviest load, was manganese which we shovelled in when the charge was pouring from the furnace to the ladle. It toughened the metal and reduced the iron oxide content in the finished steel. Ferrous silicon was also my concern, and we shovelled that into the metal to oust the gases and to help prevent blowholes in the ingots. I had also to wheel coal, the crushed anthracite kind, and stack it in paper bags, in case some recarbonisation of the metal was necessary. I had also to attend other furnaces and help in tapping the steel from them, and in repairing the empty baths. It was a busy day, for every furnace in the shop tapped its charge besides my own furnace. My last job was sweeping the whole area in front of the furnace and giving my oncoming mate the idea that a superman had been operating.

When the shift ended my furnace colleagues hinted hopefully that the newly promoted man provide the drinks. They were unlucky for I had no money. That wasn't unusual, for it was the last day before payday.

I looked forward from then onwards for more promotion days. They came at rather long intervals and I used to silently weigh up the melters' health. If they looked a bit shot at, I hoped they would stay away and give me a chance. The third-hand rate of pay was good, it depended what weekly tonnage the furnace produced, and given a keen furnace it could mean a fiver for the week.

A furnace which was very slow in production, and ready for a general rebuild, was no use at all to me, or the rest of the melters. Sometimes I got less money for working third-hand than I did at my chargewheeling job. The same thing happened when a newly rebuilt furnace was being prepared for production. About forty-eight hours were spent in what we called 'Fettling and Flowing', that covered two shifts each for the three groups of melters manning the furnace. There was a fixed rate for this non-tonnage job and it was very low. In the case of a third-hand only a few shillings.

It was a point of honour for the regular men to turn out for this period. Only there was always some one forgetting the honour and pushing spare third-hands like me in for the low paid dirty work. One didn't grumble too much, for the wheel revolved for the lucky breaks too.

While these low paid rates were not exactly injustices, our union branch officials were eternally busy having them re-formed by local agreement with the management. Our con-tention was that men were entitled to a living wage for each and every day they spent on a steel furnace.

As the war lengthened the beer got scarcer and the local publican started a rationing system. We had to queue up outside and very long queues they were too, and it took a long time to get our ration of one pint of beer. One pint was little use to men who liked ten pints and some of the heavy drinkers were reduced to queer straits. On three separate occasions and in succession, the barmaid in my pub put my pint on the counter, only for some thirsty creature to grab it up and down it.

I had never seen a pub brawl since I'd left the Beehive and I had no intention of being involved in one. So not being so fond of beer as all that, I quit the queues and the pubs, and I didn't go back until the landlords were damn glad to see anyone come in.

I have never been a great man for strong drink at any time. I can't say the same about horse betting, for it has often happened that I left a race course without having the price of a drink. The beautiful horses, the bright colours on the jocks, the racy tipsters like the late Monolulu, and the general excitement were intoxication enough for me.

I was turned twenty when I got a big lift nearer to a regular third-hand post. Three chargewheelers who were senior to me stood down from promotion. They were young, healthy and good workers but they feared continual working in heat would stiffen their limbs. In peacetime all three had been professional footballers, and hoped to resume their careers. That put me bye-turn man, which meant if only one melter lay off at any time then I went forward to third-hand. It gave me some long spells on the furnaces. On one week in particular, I caught the H. furnace at the height of its producing powers, and it ran me a pound a day. I had six pounds odd shillings to draw, and it was the very best wage I had ever earned.

By then my father had become a regular third-hand melter. It was the highest he ever attained, it was the highest he wished to be. He was fifty turned, and it needed a good fifty to stand up to such a rugged job. My brother Peter had left the cranes to become a chargewheeler too. My sister Anna Mary's frail health had sent her to live in Ireland with relatives. My mother mourned the fact, but she marvelled to think that her two sons were still with her. Not many mothers in similar situations had such fortune. If they were English mothers then not all of them wanted, they had a feeling for sacrifice. Mine had no such yen, she was just glad that we were still around. When the war ended in August 1918 I had been a regular third-hand melter for three weeks. The following month I was twenty-one years old.

11

Trade Depression

Trade was good for a long spell after the war, and that was just as we steel furnacemen expected. In our simple judgment it was steel that had torn the world apart, and steel would be needed to build it up again. Some men, reservists among them, who were called up or who joined up at the start of the war, came back to the melting shop. They had been chargewheelers before leaving, and they took their rightful positions as second-hand melters when they came back.

It was not an easy thing to do, for they had no experience at all of the hardest job in steelmaking. As second-hands they were responsible for the opening, closing, and maintenance of the tapholes. They also prepared the landers down which the steel ran into the ladles. They were responsible too for the upkeep of metal chutes and metal holes, down which, and through which, the hot iron entered the furnaces. They had to endure excessive heat in nearly every job they did, and to work mostly in cramped, awkward positions.

It was a job that called for continuity, for the continual proximity of men who gravitated without haste and without cessation, from chargewheeling to third-hands, and then on to second-hands. Without this long and widening experience the returned soldiers were facing a new enemy. Three men, Jack Fowler, Jack Young, and Jack Jones, bore it well and eventually became good first-hand melters. But Tommy Lunt lasted no time at all to his early death of pneumonia, and Jack Griffiths followed him a year or so after and with the same complaint.

The return of these men didn't affect my promotion; I wouldn't have minded if it had, but at the other end there was an exodus of the senior melters. Once the war had finished and the short-lived prosperity was still promising much, they went off to other steelworks. To me who didn't know them very well, it seemed to become a craze, something that was fashionable to do. In a short time eight first-hand melters had left us and two samplepassers.

My own good melter, Billy Lane was one; he went off to Middlesboro' and his relative, our shop manager, went with him. Billy Gale, another good melter who I respected, went off to Templeborough, and the rest vanished goodness knows where. All this provided me with many bye turn second-hand shifts, and gave me a regular position before my twenty-fourth birthday.

It was fortunate for us that our works was a modern one, it gave us a chance of partial survival when the trade slump arrived. We went along well enough until the miners came out on strike near the end of 1920. They went back after a fortnight but our complacency never came back, we knew the good times were over. On the first day of 1921 at the Work's New Year's Dance our general manager, Raymond Cooper, a fine figure in a dress suit, warned us of what lay ahead. His words came true so quickly that it seemed as if the slump had awaited in the wings for its cue. Indeed it had a long-term engagement, for it held the stage for fifteen years.

Up and down Britain it meant the end for the outdated steelworks which the war had revived; the workers in them really suffered. Where I was we never reached that stage, our place remained a steelworks and never a grass-covered heap of dismantled junk. On the melting shop we shared the work available and no one became redundant. At some periods we worked week about, one on the furnaces then one on the dole. Usually I drew a wage a little more or a little less than six pounds, and that, plus fifteen shillings unemployed pay, gave me an average of more than three pounds.

That may not look a lot but it was millions compared to

thousands of other steelworkers' incomes throughout Britain. The important thing was being on a payroll, even though it was intermittent; it was the barrier between us and despair.

There were periods when we fared better still, when we worked two full weeks for every one on the dole. We didn't experience real unemployment until the miner's strike in 1921. We depended on coal to flame the furnaces so we automatically ceased when the pits ceased producing.

I was getting on for twenty-four then, still living at home with little intention of leaving it. Like my brother Peter I was still interested in football and when he went to play for his league against a Belfast league I went with him. When we left the ship at Belfast I took money from my hip pocket to buy some coffee, and to my surprise a policeman drew a revolver. He replaced it, saying to me, 'Keep your hands out of your hip pockets if you wish to stay alive in Belfast.'

After the rest of our team had sailed for home Peter and me stayed a week in the Falls Road, the catholic quarter of Belfast. Our host was a friend who had once been a steelworker, and had gone back to his former job in an hotel. The houses were all terraced style, all old, and very much poor working class. The high-walled backyards were back to back to each other with a narrow alley in between. Without exception each wall had enough bricks removed to let a full grown person pass through. Jack Heffron, our host, said it was very necessary when the B. Specials came along. There had been a pogrom against the Catholics by the Orangemen and many had been killed and injured.

He himself had been chased one night as he and a young friend left a tramcar. Jack escaped but the other lad was battered to death. There was a nine o'clock curfew at the time and it was best to obey it. We did so too, and I found it an eerie experience living under such conditions.

Heffron's two brothers, after service in the American Navy, had come home for a holiday and they planned to go back with all the family. They were aghast at such a way of life, although they had known it of old. In the end Jack and a younger brother went with them, but try as they would they couldn't persuade their parents, or their sister to go with them.

Bullets or no bullets, or maybe because of them, there was something warm and homely and neighbourly in the Falls Road. I could well understand the Heffrons not wishing to leave it. But then I too was a Catholic so it wasn't hard for me to understand.

One day I went for a walk alone and went down a side street, and seeing a barber's shop I went in for a haircut. I was the only customer and being a perfect stranger and the times what they were, I puzzled him. A side street barber usually knows his customers.

I was still in the Catholic district so I knew that our sympathies were identical, that he was a Catholic just as I was. I had the advantage of him there and it was important for him to know. It is still important to know who you talk to in Belfast. When I put the barber at ease he said, 'you've caused a quiet stir in this street, look at them all peeping from behind their curtains.' I watched from his window and sure enough all the terraced homes I could see had some one peeping across carefully. Little did they know that they were spying on the most harmless man in Belfast.

When I reached the main road again I boarded a tramcar and went on top, and as far as the route revealed, I liked the city outskirts very much. On the way back I took a seat next to a young girl of sixteen or so, and as I glanced at her I noted an exquisite sadness in her face. I wondered at it and I noted too the way she often glanced out at the fields. I felt that she would speak to me, and she did too, 'Aren't the fields lovely and green,' she said, 'the fields of Ireland.'

Then I guessed her trouble, she was leaving the fields of Ireland and it was breaking her heart to do so. She almost broke mine as she told me that she was emigrating to America for she was lovely. If she could have stayed where she was and been mine I would have braved the Orange pogroms, coward and all though I was and a lover of safety. Better still

I could have offered her my English prospects of six months on the dole with the vague hope of being a part-time steel melter again. As it was I said little and silently wished I was going with her. I did wish her success and happiness, and although she thanked me I knew that words were no use to that girl that day.

On the following evening we left Belfast and I wasn't a bit sorry. I was going back where the people were more tolerant of my kind, even if the tolerance was only born of indifference.

The holiday feeling soon left me as my pockets grew lighter. Time, which seemed a good thing, soon palled on me for I didn't use it as wisely as my father. He was idle too but it only helped to make his days regular, and his large garden, with plenty of poultry, all the more enjoyable. The place was away a short distance from our home and his outhouses, built by himself, were comfortable enough to live in. Indeed two other plotholders, unemployed steelworkers, both did live in their outhouses. They were widowers and they found life cheaper that way.

I spent a lot of my time reading and that, in a district of practical men like in a steelworks town, can be regarded a waste of time. But there was no, or little, paid employment available, and for a short time only was it a novelty to tramp to factory and workshop and field seeking it. Continual refusals soon knocked the heart out of me, and I got a tremendously inferior feeling when bullnecked cod gaffers on building sites barked their impatient, 'Nothing doing.'

On the largest site of all, a new gasworks, about four miles away I saw my melting shop colleague, Micky McDermott, hard at it labouring. I envied him his luck first of all but as I watched I began to doubt that same luck. He was running barrow loads of wet concrete from a heap which men were mixing the hard way, with cement and sand, marble chippings and water. There were other barrow men besides Micky and running was the word for it, for they belted along almost at a gallop and across a deep hole bridged by two planks. They deposited their loads where other men were laying a floor, and returned as quickly for more concrete.

Micky nodded to me as he hurried past, there was no time for more in that chain gang. They were all Irish like himself, I could see that, and one in particular, a grim anxious sort, was always the first with his load. I went away thoughtfully; I had a question to put to Micky when he was free but I had guessed the answer already.

I met him after Mass at St Teresa's corner on the Sunday following, 'Yes,' he answered me, 'the fellow you mean gets threepence an hour extra for setting the pace and if we don't keep up we get the sack.' 'And the ganger?' I asked. 'He's Irish too,' said Micky, 'But of course you know that.' Of course I knew that and the contractor, whoever he was, knew it too, and that men be desperate to hold on to a job when times are hard.

I did not believe that the miners would win their fight but I was all for their cause. The mine owners' proposal, that the economy could only be preserved by longer hours and less money, was frightsome to me. There was no cure in deflation though the wound wouldn't have cut so deep if the coal owners had been willing to sacrifice too.

It was more than just sympathy I had for the miners, there was fear for myself, my trade, and my class. For let the miners lose their hard-won concessions and we could be next. Indeed my own firm in 1922 put forward a suggestion at a steelmaster's conference that we melters should revert back to the twelve-hour shift system. It came to nothing, for the steelmasters were never so stupid as the coal owners, but they gave nothing away and had to be watched all the time.

Our trade union too did watch them, and like hawks. All through the depression it concentrated, at the Joint Conciliation Boards, on holding on to what we had gained in the past.

I always thought that the management got away with a lot in our melting shop. The melters got absorbed so often in their steelmaking that they didn't bother to complain about many small legitimate grievances.

Though I was all for the miners I had little sympathy for

our own melting shop bricklayers when they walked out in 1922. Previous to that they had transferred from their wages system to our sliding scale method of payment. At the time the price of steel was high and that meant an immediate rise in wages. Then when the slump caused their wages to drop they demanded to go back on their previous bonus system of payment. The steelmasters refused, so out our lot went expecting sympathy from everyone and without caring what happened to the rest of us on the melting shop.

They never came back and the firm struggled through with managers and staffmen becoming bricklayers. We melters didn't help them nor did we retard them, we shut our eyes to them, for it was appalling watching them fruitlessly almost roasting themselves on maintenance jobs. In the end a new gang arose who had never served apprenticeships, but who became very proficient.

Covering the period of the miner's strike and our long idleness after it, the melting shop did not light up for six months. We asked ourselves disconsolately if it ever would. During it my only wage earning was three weeks' potato picking at four shillings a day. The farmer's son drove the digger and he all but used a whip on it, he risked his life and limb on it to keep our backs bent. The father snarled any time we straightened up, he reckoned it cost him money and that it was almost a personal insult.

Among my companions on the job were four lads from Salford. They were all about eighteen years old and had never had regular employment, and likely wouldn't until they were almost middle-aged. They were light-built little fellows, very lithe, and the monotonous back-bending didn't trouble them very much. They travelled their seven miles journey to and fro on the back of motor lorries, a frequent method of travelling during the trade depression. Each lad liked to eat a raw cabbage heart at the end of the day, by then they were almost ravenous, and they helped themselves quite openly and without thinking about our employer's grasping nature.

The farmer must have been watching and counting the number they ate and he deducted the price from their final week's wages. The boys protested but he was adamant and they had to take what he offered them. He turned away then and started walking off, parallel to a deep main drain, and the next minute the boys rushed and knocked him into it. Then they shot off like lightning and with my blessing.

The farmer was in a deplorable mess of mud and black boggy water, and could have drowned in really wet weather, for the drain was seven foot deep. I helped him out with some difficulty and with great distaste. He swore what he would do to the boys, but he had nothing to go on. He had stamped no insurance cards nor inquired for them, he didn't know their names or where they came from. I couldn't help him there and would not have done so anyway. As I walked away and left him babbling it seemed to me he was well repaid for three weeks of grouchiness and meanness.

The farm was one of a vast district of cultivated land owned by the Manchester Corporation. It provided the hedgers and ditchers and drainers and also the manure which was delivered by miniature locomotives over many miles of narrow gauge rail track. The whole area was as flat as a billiard table, and was one great market garden. In season, trains entirely loaded with lettuce left for the London market each morning.

Each day after the strike was over we steelworkers watched anxiously for smoke from the stacks. In Craigneuk we would have described it as 'Reek frae the lums,' and when at last it did come it was no brass band effort. We lit up one or two furnaces as cautiously and gingerly as if it was a top secret. The depression was letting us know that it was still in charge. I went back cautiously, and gingerly too. I was wondering if I could up to the work again. For six months of anxious idleness brought, not refreshment, but deterioration to my mind and body. However within a few weeks I was all right and back in the groove, and looking forward to my intermittent pay packet.

12

Out with the Coalminers

I rarely walked off the melting shop in those days of half capacity production without feeling sad. I missed the old robust all out, hell for leather days of the war. Then a man walked off with an air, he felt a somebody. Now it was like a bombed street with one-time furnaces, all dark and in rubble, alternating with the brightly lit ones in commission.

I was getting on, well in my twenties, and I had no money, and I was courting no girl. I seemed in a fair way to becoming a permanent bachelor. There were fellows I knew who were younger than me, and with less money than me, yet they married. I shivered at the thought, especially for those who married with not even a job to go to. They were wiser or dafter than me. I had quit playing football, for my form wasn't good with my work so exhausting, but I followed a local team. It was lively too with dances at home and away, after the matches. I spent what I had and let the week-days take care of themselves.

I got my cigarettes on tick, borrowed the price of a drink now and again from my mother. Sometimes I bet on a horse but rarely did that help me any. There was one girl I met when the team played in Ancoats, a slum part of Manchester. She was nineteen and cheerful and liked me a lot. And she was poor and a millgirl and that made me like her a lot. I felt more at home with poverty always, it was the prosperous who silenced my tongue and made me feel clumsy.

Her dance steps fitted mine and that was important, it made me still more at ease. Some times on my off weeks, when I needn't rise early, I would walk into Ancoats and take her out to the pictures. Then I'd walk home. The double journey was twenty-two miles, but I never let on, not that she could have loaned me the train fare. My father made the same journey in and out of town on most week-ends. He had found a treasure house in Shudehill's Saturday Market; he used to arrive home late at night and laden with poultry. He loved walking and scorned the lately created bus service. Once it was one o'clock in the morning when he arrived home and my mother, relieved and wrathful too, demanded, 'Why didn't you catch a bus?' He absentmindedly answered 'I was in too big a hurry to get home.'

I wasn't so fond of the walking as he was, and I was still seeing the girl in Ancoats, so I bought a cycle from Micky McDermott for five shillings plus a pair of heavy nailed working boots. The boots were a bad fit and Micky's cycle was an excellent fit. He had built it up from the melting shop scrap heap, all but the tyres. He had come back to the furnaces to this third-hand job, and had married a girl, and was hell bent on building a home. He'd ceased taking a drink and a smoke, and always sucked his pipe with it empty.

This sort of self sacrificing was awesome to me, and he intensified it when his children were born. He spent spare hours on the market gardens planting and harvesting celery and lettuce. In between signing on the Labour Exchange, he washed windows, delivered coal, clipped hedges, and concreted paths. He knew all about concreting especially, and with good reason.

I was never half so energetic as that, but the slack times were sharply separating thriving men from the dullards and there was something I had to do about it. So I went into business on Warrington Market with a fellow named Wally Stewart who was a furnaceman on the shift as myself.

We were no future business tycoons, we aimed at a pound or two to fill a habitual void and in our first efforts we managed to do so. We made ten pounds altogether dressed as Santa Claus and selling sacks full of toys at twopence a dip. Mrs Stewart made the costume and Wally and me operated on alternate days. We paid no market fees and no one asked for any, but we both possessed pedlar's licences.

Our business was something like Cinderella at the ball, it was no use after midnight Christmas Eve. I was operating that afternoon and did so well that I decided to be a real Santa Claus and give the rest of the toys away. In no time at all it seemed half the kids in Warrington were round me. I left it to them sack and all and threw the costume in for good measure.

With half of our profits Wally and me branched out as marketmen proper. We sold smallwares, 'swag stuff' was the trade slang for it, and we operated on our off weeks and well away from our homes. Our two markets, Hyde in Cheshire, and Farnworth in Lancashire were at least thirty miles away. All our stock was in two suit cases and we travelled the hard way by train and by tramcar. Sometimes in good weather we reached two pounds in profit, but in bad weather we didn't pay expenses. We didn't grumble, for often it was very interesting, and that was important, we preferred it to part-time coal delivering or clipping someone's hedges.

In fact it was not so much a pursuit of a modest profit alone but a participation in something which fascinated us. We were completely freelance; if the furnaces offered extra work, we took it gladly and resumed the markets when we were idle again. Our customers were equally freelance, they never noticed when we weren't there, at least no one ever complained to us.

In the melting shop no one ever gave any work away if he could help it; promotion, even for a day, became obsolete. If a man felt off colour he struggled along till his working period was over. If he overslept he expected someone to leave the works and knock him up. Only those who lived far out missed this service. The thought of holidays made us shiver. Since we received no holiday pay we regarded them as more idle time, and our great fear was that we wouldn't start up again.

The only man to take a holiday during the twenties was Jack Jones. He went to see his relatives in his native Rotherham and came back aghast at the poverty he witnessed. When he'd finished giving handouts he was fifty pounds down, it was all he had. No one disbelieved him for we knew him to be an open-handed fellow, but we wondered where he got his fifty pounds.

I had never heard of Jack Jones until the day he returned from the forces after the war. He walked up the shop that day with a step as lithe as a panther. He had served his time in Egypt, and had been a sergeant major. Whatever the war did to anyone else, it certainly did him good. He was five-foot-eleven, fair haired, loquacious, vital, vain, tremendously interested in everything, and the most active steel melter, mental and physical, that I ever knew.

He took a big interest in trade union affairs and in local government and soon became the best known man in the district, the most truculent, and the one with the biggest mouth. We made him our branch secretary to our very great advantage and he became a local councillor. Years later in the Labour Government of 1945 he was M.P. for Bolton and filled two minor secretaryships for different ministries.

Jones enjoyed combating the management on our behalf, He soon realised he was mentally above them, and so did his colleagues, for he told us often enough. He was an arrogant man with little humility but a surprising compassion for real hard cases, and that cost him money he couldn't afford.

Once he said to me, 'Fellows like you, Paddy, when you've anything to say to the management you go trembling and with your cap in your hand. You never let yourself find out that you may be better than any of them.'

So far as I was concerned it was strictly true, but I was glad Jack found out, for he wrested many a bright pound for us in local payment rates.

Jones was emotional; one moment his deep baritone would be competing with the charging machines and the next he'd be sunk in gloom. One Sunday morning he frightened the life out of me for a moment or two, he was sitting near his furnace, weeping bitterly, and threatening to commit suicide. He had publicly denounced some local council official as a thief and the fellow was threatening to sue him. Only then was Jack remembering that all he had was an intermittent pay packet, which had to be earned first, and a wife and six kids who were all as healthy as trouts.

I didn't know what the devil to do, I wasn't used to weeping men who threatened to destroy themselves, I was just pondering some consolatory words when Jack's furnace had a say in the matter, the charge inside reacted and sent a huge flame blazing through the furnace doors. It also belted the white hot slag all over the floor.

That was Jones' chance if he had really wished to die then all he needed was to stay where he was. In a few seconds he would have been just a cinder, but he didn't, instead he up and flew like the wind, and I did too.

We had to shovel it all up, just the two of us, for we were on a watching shift which meant the full furnace complement wasn't completed. We were soaked in sweat long before we finished and it soaked some sense into him too, for there was no more talk of suicide.

The council official never sued Jones and a while afterwards I heard Jack declare that the fellow 'was as guilty as hell'. He saw me looking at him but it never registered, he was in one of his up periods.

Jones had a fixation about nationalisation of the steel trade. His brain, energised by the suns of Egypt, so he declared, could see how the workers had been duped. 'Look,' he said, 'we won the war, we had twelve months of false prosperity and since then a deluge of misery. Man-made misery created by that old fox Lloyd George. The control of steel, of coal, and of the railways was in the government's hands and what did it do? It dropped them like hot potatoes so to keep the working class chained'. 'Yes,' I answered, 'but nationalisation can't prevent depression in trade. If there is no market then how can we sell our steel?' Jones said ex-

E

pansion instead of deflation would open up the market, and that nationalisation instead of isolation would increase our technology and so help us compete with the world.

'Aren't we competing with the world as it is?' Smudger Smith asked him. Jones replied, 'Not much or with anyone else. Look how little we turn out here and we're busy compared to other places.' Big Johnny Hetherington wanted to know if nationalisation would give us a pension. He was forty years old and senior second-hand in age as well as in line of promotion. He had been twenty-one years on steel furnaces, first in Scotland and then in England, and very likely the question was prompted by the knowledge that his youth had passed. Jones told him that nationalisation would surely facilitate pensions and that the time was coming when all worthwhile trades would have worthwhile pensions.

Pensions for steelworkers was something I never thought of for I was young at the time, and inclined to scorn humdrum safety precautions in old age. But Jones' words did make me realise that with pensions or without them, steel furnacemen could live to grow old as well as men in any other walk of life. The eight-hour shifts and machine charging furnaces had done that for us. I remembered too that in Craigneuk, with its twelve hours every shift on hand-charged furnaces, I had never heard or known a furnaceman who had lived to be old, really and truly old.

Jack Jones was not exactly a John the Baptist preaching nationalisation in a wilderness. The rest of us were interested, only milder. Despite our Confederation's exhortations we remained mild and never became enthusiastic. It was a poor time for enthusiasms and we might have responded better, more vehemently, if we had hated more. But ours wasn't a hating trade, steelmaking in Britain never has been a hating trade. The end products are tough, but its practitioners are mild.

The coalminers made up for us; they had plenty to hate, especially in the twenties, a grim decade for them. Their misery as near as dammit, had all but triggered a general strike in 1921 and 1925. It did just that in May 1926 and gave Britain the weirdest nine days it ever had. From May 4th till May 12th, it seemed like a malevolent dream world to me, a sort of nightmare civil war. I saw the amateur engine drivers, and bus drivers in Manchester, and watched amateur constables create chaos miles long in the city streets, and I thought in wonder, 'These men and me are on different sides, we are enemies.'

Yet I saw nothing of the government's emergency preparations, and I saw no trouble. We steelworkers quit immediately, and when the General Council of Trade Unions called off the strike, we stayed out with the miners. Not in sympathy alone; we couldn't have restarted any way, for while the mines were closed we lacked the coal necessary for steelmaking.

It was a very good summer that year and that at least was helpful, but it was all over and into November, and even December, before the miners gave in, and beaten on all points.

I was twenty-nine in the September after the General Strike and I was still unmarried and with no prospects. With months of unemployment behind me and more months of it in front of me I hadn't a penny to my name. My clothes were so worn and shabby that I felt ashamed to meet acquaintances who were employed. I felt the sight of me embarrassed them and that they might embarrass me by offering money to me. Sometimes I hated these people so much for their good fortune that I grew alarmed at my state of mind.

I was far more at ease with steelworkers unemployed like myself, and sensibly we formed a dramatic society. I found out I had the makings of a tolerably good actor and I wasn't surprised. I also joined W.E.A. classes and one subject in particular, the history of the Lancashire cotton trade, interested me greatly. Yet up to then, when at work on the furnaces, I had never given a thought to such studies.

These activities kept my brain working in pleasant channels and brought me in contact with intelligent women.

Their very intelligence would have made me shyer than ever, it did do at first, but their easy unself-consciousness was contagious, and I enjoyed their company immensely, They set me thinking of the girl in Ancoats, I had lost touch with her for months and wondered if she had married. The thought kept troubling me, and that I must find out, for she was the one girl I felt really happy with. So I wrote to her and I was delighted to hear that she was single, free, and would be glad to see me again.

I walked into Manchester, took her to a picture house, had tea at her home, and walked the whole way back. I had let my cycle go rusty but from then on it went into commission, for I wanted to see that girl again.

It was turned 1927 before we stepped on the melting shop again. I had no regular work since the previous May, and neither had the other melters save for a lucky handful. Wally Stewart and me had ceased our market trading. We had ran out of capital, and besides Wally had landed a ferryman's job on the Ship Canal. The day I went to see him he was winching a car across on the floating platform. I gave a hand to wind the cable on the drum and when I offered my penny fare Wally refused it. 'You've worked your passage,' he told me generously.

He untied the ferry boat from the platform and sculled us back again. I left him there leaning on his pole and waiting for two ladies to step on the boat. As he waited he said dreamily, 'I often wonder what it's like to have a shore job.' That made me laugh all the way to the main road again.

In the late summer I had two weeks work on a thrashing machine at four and sixpence a day. Then in the October I went to my standby the potato picking, but with a different farmer and at five shillings a day. At home we missed no meals, especially when my father landed a job with a road-making firm. A wonderful event, for he was in his sixtieth year, but still hardy and strong. Better still there was another vacancy and the boss asked my father to bring someone along.

My heart leapt at the news, for I felt it was mine, but he disillusioned me in the nicest possible way. For only that morning had his friend first failed to turn up on their job-seeking expeditions. He felt this man, who was middle-aged and with family responsibilities, had the first chance. I agreed unhappily, but not unwillingly, and admired my father more than ever, for what under the circumstances was a most generous act. His friend of course was glad of the job and stayed with the firm for the rest of his working lifetime.

I couldn't help longingly thinking of that job through the months that followed, especially after meeting the girl in Ancoats again. The difference it would have made and the chance it would have provided for saving and marriage. When I drew my first pay packet from the furnaces I started to save in real earnest.

13

Ireland

Alas for my plans, in my third week back on the furnaces I had to quit. My heart was strained through repeated physical exhaustion of the previous years. At Ancoats hospital a specialist told me that only rest and freedom from worry would cure it. 'Apart from that', he said, 'you haven't a trace of disease in your body.'

It was bad news and good news but his advice was submerged in a monstrous depression. I had taken my heart for granted and had never given it a thought, but from then on I thought of nothing else. I feared every moment that I would drop dead and I could not sleep in the night on account of those fears. My strength left me so much that each morning I despaired of the day ahead. My parents, especially my mother, must have been heart sick of me; an illness was bad, but to continually moan about it was very selfish of me.

I still went into Ancoats to see my girl and often walked each way despite my weakness. I never took her anywhere, I couldn't afford it, but it never upset her. She took no notice when I sadly told her that she would be far better without me, but remained cheerful and hopeful. If her widowed mother and sister had any doubts about her wisdom they never revealed it to me, I was always welcome and they asked no questions.

After three months away from work and feeling not a bit better, I realised that complete change was my one hope. I knew where to go and my father loaned me the money, and I'm sure was glad to be rid of me. So I packed my very few possessions and a day or so after and I was in Ireland, on my

Uncle Terry's little farm in the hills of Armagh. I had known Terry when I was a boy in Craigneuk, for he had various spells on the steelworks there and had always quit in the springtime to go back and put in his crops and to cut the peat. He was an easy-going man, but so were they all in Granemore, and that despite tilling the stoniest land in all Armagh.

My uncle had married a fine thriving woman and they had built a well-stocked general store to the farmhouse. The neighbours didn't call him Terry, they called him, 'Big Lazy Tar', and that made him grin and move slower than ever. Compared to many he was well-doing, not a strong farmer as the Irish have it, but able to manage nicely. The peat stack near the house was large and neat, his two cows healthy, and Nelly his young mare well able to pull the bright yellow and blue painted cart from the bog.

The worst calamity that could happen to any home in Granemore was to lose a cow, for the greater percentage of families owned but one. If the cow died it meant the loss of milk and butter until such times as it could be replaced. Or it would have done but for the communal system which had existed from away before the great potato famine of 1846. There was no question of totting up a lengthening bill by the neighbours, they provided the milk and butter freely, knowing well that their misfortune would receive the same consideration.

'With one good cow and the land to graze it, and a strip for cabbages and potatoes, and a few hens roaming around and laying at home, and that's all we need for life in Granemore,' said a woman to me one day. She was proving the truth of it every day, and the strong sweet tea and the well buttered soda bread I partook proved she had something to spare besides.

Although I was but one generation from this way of life I felt I was twenty times farther away from it. It never occurred to me that one cow could be the mainstay of a family. No wonder the animals were regarded with affection, attention, and anxiety. Contrary to many an ill-informed English opinion, I never saw any of them or any pigs in the kitchen. I'd have been very surprised if I had.

The countryside was beautiful for it was springtime, and the roads were narrow and winding with little ups and downs all the way. From some points I could see my uncle's home and so high up that it seemed on the slope of the Brague mountain. The people called it a mountain though hill would have been a better description.

I loved the sight of the hills, I never realised it before but they were a necessity to my mental and physical wellbeing. They filled me with peace from the mornings when I first looked out at them till the evenings when the dark enveloped them. I loved the sweet silence, it was balm after the noise and rattle and crash of my steelworks existence. Often late at night I would walk home through a white mist and feeling as if I was the only soul on earth. As lonely as that and loving it because it was so different from the loneliness of cities. Since it would be late and my relatives asleep I used to always hold the tail of their big friendly collie, else as it swished to and fro the chairs went flying.

Very few seemed to go to bed early in Granemore, for the bright oil lamps beckoned through the dark like lighthouses. Nor did they rise early in the mornings, for I usually stepped out at eight o'clock and I had the whole countryside to myself. But awake or not, there would be a thin blue spiral of peat smoke arising from the chimneys, for the fires never went out. Each night before retiring the last job was to bank the fires with rough peat sods. All through the night they would burn slowly, and in the morning, a puff of the fan bellows would sparkle the blaze for the fire to be built up again.

Although my Aunt Ellen sold matches in her store I never saw a Granemore man buy any or use any. Bidding her the time of day, they would walk in from the road, lift a glowing ember with the tongs, and press it to the pipe bowl. Always there would be tea in the pot, and they would refresh themselves and linger a while if the talk was good. If it was extra good, they might postpone their original intention of working, until after dinner.

Conversation in Granemore was regarded as an art; the good conversationalist was respected and listened to. I heard words and phrases and sentences like polished jewels coming from the lips of men with little education or book reading. It was extra welcome to me after the dreary, limited, and often filthy language of the steelworks.

The leisured pace for me was truly just what the doctor ordered. The spring passed, and before it did I helped my uncle Terry cut the peat in the bog. Each day I grew stronger in a land where everyone had the civil word. I walked plenty and when I was thirsty I'd call at any house for a drink of buttermilk, which is the best thirst quencher in the world. When I was tired I would climb into some farmer's cart as it went on its way to Keady town, or to the bog. Once I travelled that way with a sad kind man and we talked of health. 'Only health counts,' I said. 'That's true indeed,' he agreed with gentle melancholy,' but sure it doesn't last.' We both fell silent and I was thinking his words were the saddest I had ever heard.

Lack of money didn't trouble me in Granemore as it did in England. No one else had any and there were no fine shops to set me longing. The only money I had was from the National Health and I turned it over intact to my aunt and hoped it would be enough. I had but rarely the price of a stamp and I was often tempted to steal a packet of cigarettes from my aunt's store. I didn't do it but I was never proud of my forbearance for failure always seemed imminent, just waiting around the corner.

Angela Trodden was a fine looking girl, and the daughter of John Trodden the man I respected most in Granemore. Their home was my favourite visiting place and although John was very old he was the master and was obeyed without dispute. One time when Angela, on reaching her doorstep after a four-miles walk from Keady town, remembered she had forgotten old John's weekly newspaper, she turned right round and walked all the way back. I was glad it was her decision and not mine; I was glad of the newspaper too for John and me read every item and discussed it all night. Alice was the oldest of the two girls, she was twenty-two and Angela was twenty. Their only brother Peter Augustus was twenty-four and their father who had married late in life was well over seventy.

Alice was married and she and her baby were marking time in her father's home, while her husband in Glasgow, provided one for them. Peter Augustus despite his impressive christian names was the least imposing of the family. He was medium height, tanned almost black, and had little conversation for anyone. He had least of all with old John who gave him his orders every morning and left it at that. The girls treated him with similar brevity, but there was no sign of ill nature and Peter Augustus never resented it. All the same I was hard put to regard Peter as a member of the family at all.

He was respected throughout Granemore as a hardworking man and I believed it, although he didn't hurry any more than the rest. I saw him in action in the bog when he was peat cutting. I had gone with him and the two girls and I was prepared to help for I was feeling much better. The pure air was good for me and I liked working in the bog, I thought it the healthiest work on earth.

Peter Augustus used the specially shaped spade for peat cutting, slane was its name in Granemore, and the girls and me lifted the brick-shaped pieces and laid them in rows upended to dry. It needed little force for the slane to cut through the soft peat bank, and Peter Augustus didn't hurry but neither did he slack his pace. With his pipe steadily drawing he was a picture of lean, tanned muscularity.

As usual he was silent but Angela made up for him, as she watched like a hawk for the first sign of me tiring. She was a mocking, jibing, bitch of a girl, and I longed to throw her in the black bog water at the foot of the peat bank. I doubted

very much if her brother Peter Augustus would have bothered to stop me, but I felt certain that she was strong enough to
throw me in.

In truth my back was hurting plenty but I wasn't letting
her know that. Hour after hour Peter Augustus worked; he
paused only to knock the ash from his pipe, then at it again
like a machine. Back home on the furnaces we were human
enough to straighten up for a breather but this fellow was the
limit. Yet he wasn't trying to be big in front of me. He was
just a sturdy peasant operating in his native element, and it
was important to keep going while the weather was good.

It was Angela who broke first, and wasn't I glad. 'We'll
eat, boys,' she said, and soon we had a fire of dried peat going.
We had boiled eggs, two each, and farls of soda bread well
buttered, and strong sweet tea in mugs. A feast for gods.

That evening as I walked the three long miles from the bog
I was as weary as an old horse. It was good though to hear
Angela sincerely congratulate me on my effort. It was not
my professional field of endeavour and I wasn't quite match
fit, but the old furnace endurance had proved useful. All the
same I felt mortified to hear next day that Angela and Peter
Augustus had spent the whole night dancing in Micky
Lappin's barn. I had been simple enough to imagine that
they were as tired as me.

After a few weeks of dry weather Peter, Angela and me
went back to the bog to 'foot the turf'. This meant upending
the pieces in groups of four with them leaning against each
other to catch the sun and the wind. A lot of the moisture had
already left them and they reminded me of chunks of thick
black tobacco. In a month or so after that, given some decent
weather, the peat was thoroughly dry, and we stacked it in
rows near the bog road. It was the handiest way for the
Troddens to come and cart it home. There was no hurry for
that, for once the peat was dried it remained dried; the rain
would slide off its hardened outer skin like glass.

In July I had two letters from England that pleased me
well. One from my girl Aileen in Ancoats who had saved the

fare and was coming to see me, and to see Ireland for the first time. I resolved to go back with her, for my other letter contained ten pounds. It was from Jack Jones, our trade union secretary, and it was a grant due to me for long standing absence through sickness.

I was sorry to leave Granemore and the kind people in it but very glad that I had been there. There were other things to do now and I was anxious once more to have a try at them. The day after we returned I went to the melting shop and told the management I would start back the next day.

14

Marriage

When I walked up the melting shop the next afternoon some of the morning turn wished me good luck. I needed it too, for my furnace had just tapped and I was right in at the hottest part of the job. In three minutes flat I went to relieve my mate.

He was a busy little man and an aggrieved one, for his colleagues, in their hurry to get ready for home, had deserted him. When I reached him at the back of the furnace he was lashing shovelfuls of manganese into the streaming metal and talking to himself, cursing his mates I supposed. He was swinging blindly with his face averted from the fierce heat but he was finding his target all right. His name was Eli Newton and he was a very excitable little man and a very good melter.

'Off you pop, Eli,' I said and taking the shovel from his hand. He let it go and when he saw it was me he grabbed it back, saying, 'Take it easy Paddy. Why, God's truth, man, you've been away a lifetime, leave it to me.' So I did just that and he had finished a moment or two afterwards. He had plenty to tell me but I didn't know what he was talking about. It was all about tapholes and metal holes, and what he had done and what the other man should have done and didn't. Eli always spluttered that way and I would soon get used to him again. When he finished talking he hurried off and then scampered back again, 'I almost forgot,' he said breathlessly, 'how are you feeling Paddy?' Before I could answer he was off again. I smiled to myself, he was the same old Eli sure enough.

I turned and lifted a fire hook from the cooling bosh, just to get the feel of it again. As I did so the ladle crane driver swung his auxiliary over for me to hook the chain on to the lander. On the other side of the lander a third-hand melter, his face protected by his sweat towel, also hooked a chain. I followed suit, for the heat was terrific, and the day itself in high summer was very warm. The third-hand hooked his chain smartly and stepped away rapidly. I fumbled mine in my newness, recovered it, tried again, missed it again, and then managed it. I breathed in the hot gassy air with relief, for it seemed that I might make a melter again. I had worried about that many a time and I would know better by the end of the shift.

The crane moved off to the nearby moulds with the ladle of steel clamped in the huge arms of the main hoist and the long end of the lander swinging high on the auxiliary chains. The liquid, all slag now, still poured from the furnace tap-hole, down the short lander and into the slagholes below. I put on my protective gloves and picked up a heavy steel sheet about six feet long and four feet in breadth and dropped it in the space vacated by the long lander, and just clear of the flowing slag. When the time came I was ready for sealing the taphole again, so that the furnace could proceed to the next charge.

By this time the rest of my colleagues had arrived and the second-hands and third-hands had come to help out in the usual communal fashion. Judging by the throng it seemed that I would have very little to do, although I was willing to try, but my mates, Jack Jones, Mick Loftus, Artie McGowan, and Smudger Smith shouldered the burden of my work on that first day. The other three second-hands, Big Johnny Hetherington, Tommy Clark and Michael Bennett, were laid off that week. They signed on the dole and resumed the furnaces the following week. It was 1927 and the trade depression had still years to go.

On the front side of the furnace where my first-hand Barry Starrs, and my third-hand Louis Doyle, toiled at the fettling along with the two chargewheelers, Harry Green and Billy Waterhouse, they were just as considerate, my work was their work for that day. On the morrow, and all the other tomorrows I would be climatised and ready for anything. WHEN THE DAY ENDED I FELT TIRED BUT UN-AFRAID, I WAS A MELTER AGAIN.

The samplepasser too wished me luck; he was a big, handsome, overwhelming fellow named Bert Leadbetter, and a different kind entirely from Freddy Hall my previous one. Leadbetter acted in his own small world like an emperor, and was treated like one by the furnacemen and by the melting shop management too. He was the complete practical steelmaker, a proud man who led a middle-class life outside, had his car and his golf club, his fine house and family, and a shrewd interest in the stock market. His son David once told me that he was, 'the most self-centred man in the World', and I well believed it. He got away with things at that time and age that neither he, nor any other boss, would dare do after the second world war.

'Big Bert,' which was all he ever got, was forgiven much for his huge sense of humour. It was a pleasure to tell him a good story or to make a witty remark, his appreciation was instantaneous and his laughter was long and generous. When there was nothing to thwart him at home or abroad, then he was the sunniest tempered and gayest companion in the world. When he was upset his merciless tongue could shrivel a man in a way he would never forget.

Since he was the emperor he made his kings, and he trained them well. Donnelly, Thornton, Tom Gallagher, Sen. McGowan, Blane, all of them became samplepassers and good, calm knowledgeable men. He never tried to make anything of Wally Stewart or me, we were his court jesters. I was a witty man and so was Stewart, and we were a lot more important to the 'sucker-ups' than they ever realised.

After a few months of work and the dole, my marriage plans took shape somewhat. Then a terrible setback occurred. My brother Peter had done well at the greyhound tracks. It was a new gambling sport from America, and out of his winnings he bought a racing greyhound and placed it with a trainer on a Manchester track. So one night when it was considered unbeatable I put my savings on it. It didn't win and I was back where I started. It still was supposed to be unbeatable on the following three occasions and each time I borrowed money to bet on it, and each time the unbeatable got beat. That made it worse than ever, I now had to pay back what I owed, before I could get back where I started.

Sadly I returned to the hard way, and in the meantime when I wasn't looking, the greyhound turned out and won at the odds of 10-1. I shouldered this blow with the rest of them and in silence. I was a stoic because I didn't wish any one to know how daft I'd been and above all I didn't wish my girl to know. It set me back some months and I perjured my soul with the lying excuses I conjured up. Altogether I was anything but proud of myself, and it was with great relief that I finally acquired twenty pounds. So I married my girl and if I didn't live happy ever after then it wasn't her fault. I do know that it was the best thing that ever happened to me.

We lived in Ancoats first of all with my wife's mother and sister, and on one of my idle weeks we spent our honeymoon in Ireland in Granemore. We had quite a few nice presents and one of the nicest thoughts came from Tommy Clark my colleague on the furnaces. He suggested to the other second-hands that I should miss a turn on the laying off rota. That would have meant four weeks consecutive pay packets before hitting the dole queue again. A prodigious affair at such a time, and I was grateful to Tommy indeed. Big Johnny Hetherington, Smudger Smith, Mick Loftus, and Michael Bennett agreed willingly but Jack Jones and Arthur McGowan refused. They were intelligent men who knew that their actual loss would be trifling and I fought them on it and hard too, but they beat me. Under an easy-going exterior they were as flinty as rocks.

Living in Ancoats was a novelty to me, although the going

and coming added two hours to my working day. Instead of steelworkers it was a change to have organ-grinders, and Italian ice cream merchants, for neighbours. The family next door to me lived well from operating a bird stall in the Shudehill Saturday Market. At certain times and always on Sunday mornings the father and two sons travelled into Cheshire to trap songbirds. The man next to them was a bookmaker's runner, and two doors further down was the home of a burglar. A poor one at his profession, for he was mostly in jail. I didn't see him once in the years I lived there. He had a phobia for stealing hams, and only from the local wholesale grocers, so when he had a haul it was a short-lived one, the police went straight to his door. His name was Billy Lumb and I heard he was a likeable man. When he died, all the Manchester newspapers gave a sympathetic account of him and his ill-chosen career.

On my idle weeks I used to sign on the dole at Aytoun Street Labour Exchange in the centre of Manchester. I heard say that forty thousand of us queued up there every week for our government allowance. That was in the years 1928, 29, 30, when the world depression was on. The slow movement in the twice weekly queues occupied hours of my time, but I never minded, in fact I regarded it as part of my social life. Men talked as they shuffled along and it was often very interesting, and sad too.

I think the dole ran me eighteen shillings a week at that time. I didn't claim for my wife Aileen and we had no family. I know that there were men drawing that sum and existing strictly within it. They were single men of various ages, and they lived in dosshouses in the Oldham Road. It was a grey life indeed and the malnutrition showed in their faces. It was doubtful, even if good times came, that they could ever become whole men again.

One man there, a van driver, told that he had recently landed a job but he only lasted a fortnight. The long lay-off previously with its poverty and anxiety had shaken his nerves so that he couldn't face the traffic. He told me sadly that his employer, a considerate man, just dare not risk him any longer.

Usually after leaving the labour exchange I crossed Portland Street and sat on the Piccadilly benches. All kinds of people sat there and I always looked for the down and outs, the unemployed who had become unemployable. Most of them were transients, resting and gathering strength to go on to nowhere. It was hard to speak to them, for they were lonely men used to silence, and the offer of a shilling or two caused no elation, as likely as not it would be refused. They had got beyond the stage when anything mattered and very few of them were sane. It was no wonder indeed.

When I'd leave Piccadilly Gardens as like as not I would cut up Stevenson's Square on my way home. It was a favourite place then for ex-servicemen's bands and choral groups. I always looked out for one particular lot, eight in number, each of whom had lost a limb. They were all powerful men with an extremely outdoor, well-fed, contented look about them, and their deep voices competed successfully with the city's clamour. Their collecting bag was always well filled.

Ancoats was not a healthy place, its housing was terrible, its poverty plentiful, but in it were lots of people who had lived to be old and cheerful with it. They were good advertisements for no luxury, plenty hardship, and just-enough-to-eat existences. I liked to talk to them and I always remember one old lady giving me her life history in two minutes flat. It was all the time I could spare, for I was hurrying to catch the afternoon train to work. She was following a loaded coal cart up the cobbled George Leigh street and picking up any piece that jolted off. She was completely delighted when I gave her a shilling. There was no self-pity about her, no bitterness, but a glint of humour as she winded up, 'So here I am and scratching for a living like an old hen.'

Manchester in the morning pleased me, I loved to see the city asleep as I walked through it at five o'clock when on the early morning turn. I loved too to see it awakening when I walked off the Central Station when returning from night-shift.

A small group of steelworkers, about six or seven of us, always travelled to and fro. That wasn't so much for friend-ship as it was protective, for travelling alone in working clothes among well-dressed passengers was embarrassing. We didn't feel tough even if we looked so for working men are actually the most harmless of people. It was always a compliment to us when nervous ladies travelling alone realised our harmlessness and entered our compartment.

I made use of the city to cloak some of my own affairs. I'd become slightly acquainted with an ice cream manufacturer named Rice, a Manchester-born Italian whose business was just round the corner from me. He made the ice cream and rented out the tubs in handcarts, complete with biscuits and utensils. He suggested that I worked for him in my idle weeks.

I did so four times and made between thirty shillings and two pounds profit each occasion. I had luck with the weather and I pushed my handcart as far as Newton Heath, about two miles away, and selling as I went along. I was relaxed enough at this unusual occupation for me because nearly all my customers were children. I never told a word of my experiences to my workmates; somehow steelmaking and selling ice cream seemed incompatible.

We lived in Ancoats for five years for a home nearer my job, not right back to the steelworks district but one railway station away from it. A lot happened during the years in Ancoats. Our first child Kevin Peter was born and died there while still an infant. My wife was ill for long time but recovered completely. My mother died, and that was the greatest blow, for I wondered how my father would fare without her. He took it sensibly, peacefully, and kept his grief to himself. My sister Anna Mary kept house for him, and there were only the two of them, for my brother Peter had married and was living near the steelworks. My father was still on the melting shop but had quit the furnaces for a light labouring job. He was sixty-six when we left Ancoats and I was thirty-six and I was in good trim, and lean after the fashion of most steel melters.

I had some money in the bank; that was nothing wonderful but the determination which put it there was an unusual feature for me. Trade was still dull but that year, 1933, was far better for our trade than the previous one. There were plenty far worse off than we were and when we read the newspapers we wondered how we fared so well.

15

Nightshift Moods

For working men like me the great trade depression was like entering a tunnel in 1921 and slowly traversing it until a gleam in 1934 told us that at last we were nearing the daylight.

If I had a reason at all for gratitude to the depression it was for missing so many months of nightshifts. There were periods lasting a year or more when my quota of work was on the morning and afternoon shifts with the nightshift week free to sign on the dole.

If I had to lose work and wages then those were the weeks for me, for I heartily disliked working in the night. The only misery to equal it, in my opinion, was trying to get restful sleep in the daytime. They were corollary to each other, two demons propping each other up.

The afternoon shift I like and always did. I arrived home from it early enough to find my household still awake and I retired at my leisure. I slept well and long and I rose at my leisure. The morning shift meant very early rising, but it was worth it for the sake of its early finish and free evenings. It was the one week when we lined up with the dayworkers, when we lost for a short while that sense of isolation which many shift workers experience.

We were not all similar in our approach to shiftwork, some of my mates disliked the afternoon turn and preferred the night turn to it. No one grumbled at the early morning turn and many would have worked it constantly if it had been possible. A few liked the night turn most and even one or two of them would have taken it over constantly. They were the people who could lay their heads on the pillows and sleep soundly through the daytime for seven, eight, nine hours. They rose up always refreshed with good digestions, good tempers, and went out happily for some more night work. They also listened in wonder to any one burbling about being unable to catch sleep in the daytime.

I always placed regular night workers in a different category to the shift workers. I knew plenty, and none of them steelworkers, and they always seemed happy men. They defended their method of earning a living, and most of them had deliberately sought continual night work. There were many reasons. It fitted in better with their domestic affairs; it paid better wages than day work; it was free from noise and bustle, or it may have helped them escape unpleasant foremen. All such benefits notwithstanding they were welcome to constant night work, I had no ambition to share it with them.

Yet if anyone was a natural for shift work, surely it was me. Since I was first able to look around me I saw men coming and going on shifts. I do not believe it ever affected my health, or that it affected the health of any steelworker, provided they started it when they were young. I do know that the nightshift affected tempers, so that many men were very hard to live with. It didn't break homes up but it hushed them up. Anxious wives tiptoed through the home in the daytime, and it was hard for the children to realise that the moody silent man upstairs in the bedroom was the cheerful father they knew on the day turn.

I was a stinker at home, until I hammered out a philosophy that gave me some measure of peace, and my family too. When at last I realised that I would never possess that mysterious affinity to sound daytime sleep, I ceased to pursue it. I would fray my nerves no longer by continually chasing it, instead I would be satisfied with rest. So I read my books and my magazines and newspapers in bed and when they fell from my hands I dozed a little, for fifteen minutes, thirty minutes, an hour, and then back to my books again. Before long I would doze over again for another short period of half slumber. In that way I found rest.

Other men who were not readers evolved their own system of partial salvation. Some found that a midday drink in their usual pub could send them home to a sleepful afternoon. Whichever way we managed, we were the men who didn't like nightshift, the ones who drifted through it, and who always welcomed the end of it.

At times I suffered more from other men's inadequacies than from my own. Barry Starrs, the first-hand I worked with for a long time, could be a tartar on the nightshift. He frequently stripped his home of electric light bulbs, leaving his family in darkness, or so he hoped. Though I fancied his family would have some stored away after the first time.

Having made this asinine start he would brood about it. It was uncomfortable for the rest of us, and since he gave the orders we knew what to expect. When tapping time came, our most exhausting and busy period, he would deliberately hang up the job instead of getting it over swiftly and surely. The extra burden fell upon himself too as well as the rest of us, but he endured that because the black mood was on him. He soaked Louis Doyle, his third-hand, and me so much and so often, that we were like greyhounds, just as lean but not as swift. We were both fit men and gruelling periods were nothing new to us, but this was different: it came from stupidity and meanness and we resented it greatly.

Often at the end of such a night Doyle and me would be hard put for the strength to stagger home. For there comes a condition after excessive sweating in great heat when there is almost nothing left. The eyes stare fixed and dead, the voice whispers from spent lungs, and the limbs move with a leaden weight. We would sit in the cabin recruiting our battered resources while Starrs, grim and unlovely as ever, would mutter to any who cared to listen, 'Look at those Irish bastards over there plotting murder and rebellion.'

When week-end arrived with its welcome rest and its

changeover to the early morning turn we'd see a new first-hand on the furnace, a man full of good fellowship and generosity. A man who was anxious to please and have us forget the atrocious character he had presented on nightshift. We'd forgive him readily, we would have done anything for this pleasant courteous fellow. All would be grand until the next nightshift week and then the same old game would start all over again. Once more his family would hate the sight of him, and once again Louis Doyle and me would become a couple of sweat-drenched Irish bastards. Poor old Starrs. He's dead long ago and he wasn't a bad fellow at all but for the nightshift.

Indeed Bert Leadbetter was just as bad when the night-shift mood was on him, and since he was the boss we had to put up with it. We didn't need to, we could quit if we wanted, but the dole queue for regular had a deucedly hungry look about it. That was the only alternative the times offered.

When nightshift blues got hold of Bert the word went round the place like lightning. Each man muttered to the other, 'Watch your step, the big fellow has got them on him.'

It was good advice and rarely neglected except when Barry Starrs was in one of his extra particulars. Then mood met mood, blackness met blackness, like two vast bulls inter-locking. One time about midnight Bert came along to the furnace, glanced inside to note progress, then said contemptuously to Starrs, 'Give her lime, man. Can't you see the slag is too thin?' Then he walked on leaving Starrs frothing at the mouth at this slur on his steelmaking ability. 'I'll give her lime,' he said grimly to Louis Doyle and me, 'fetch the charging machine.' We both hugged ourselves inwardly, one grasped at any diversion to counter the monotony of night-shift, and this promised to be real good.

The charging machine started ramming the lime into the furnace and didn't stop until a whole ten tons wagon load went in. The liquid charge underneath was buried beneath a mountain of it. To a furnaceman it was an appalling sight and it would take hours and hours before it fluxed into the slag. Starrs in his blind rage had set the furnace back six hours.

The damage done, he donned his jacket and raincoat, slung his haversack over his shoulder, and said to me, 'Paddy, tell Mr Leadbetter she's had the lime, and tell him to work the bloody charge himself.' With that he walked into the night and made for his home four miles away. Bert Leadbetter was a very angry man when he viewed the mess, 'The fool has sacked himself this time for sure,' he said. It looked that way, Starrs in his fearful temper had kicked a fifteen pound a week job through the window. At a time too when thousands were signing on the dole, and unemployed men were marching in protest to the government representatives in London.

I took over the furnace for the rest of the night. I had Charlie Nicholls, the charging machine driver, scoop out what lime he could with his deft handling; that helped a little, and he levelled the rest of it fairly evenly. When the lime was thoroughly hot I had Charlie spread two boxes of iron oxides over it. 'It will flux some day,' I told myself. At that moment I had little hope of getting the charge in condition before quitting at six o'clock. But I was wrong, for to my satisfaction and Bert Leadbetter's too we had it sizzling in the ladle just as the day turn men were walking up the shop.

'I wonder what that big ass thinks of himself now,' said Bert thoughtfully to me. I had an answer ready, not a very witty one, but fortunately he thought it was, 'I don't know,' I said, 'but I'll bet his wife and kids are refugees by now.' Bert laughed heartily and I chanced the really important question, 'What about him? I'll be passing his way this afternoon.' 'Good,' answered the big fellow, 'Tell the fool to turn out tonight as usual.'

A very subdued Barry Starrs was much relieved to hear it.

16

Easing the Burden

While it was true that the relationship between masters and
men was comparatively good in the steel trade, we watched
each other like hawks nevertheless, and during the depression especially. The brotherhood of man would have taken
many a bashing but for the vigilance of our Confederation.

The mistaken palliation of reduced wages and increased
hours of labour was eternally threatening to put us right back
in the late nineteenth century again. Our Confederation itself had suffered severely in loss of income and membership,
and at a time when the employers were amalgamating. My
own firm became a member of a corporation in 1930 and
with the aid of the Bank of England set off on an extended
plan of modernisation. This included a new blast furnace,
coke ovens, rolling mill, and steel furnaces of one hundred
tons producing capacity.

That was good for us, but it was bad for the Wigan iron
and steelmakers within the amalgamation, for it closed them
down. So many of the Wigan men travelled the twelve miles
journey to and from the melting shop whenever a furnace
required rebuilding. This meant three or four weeks work,
and then back on the dole again until another furnace went
down for repairs. The result was that the Wiganer at home
kept his ears to the ground listening for the sound of falling
furnaces twelve miles away.

Wigan had a very rough time during the depression, and
it showed in the eager way their men tackled a job. They
streamed off the workmen's trains and through the station
subway like harriers. An unthinking man going in the op-

posite direction would have been swept into the middle of the steelworks before he freed himself.

When trade improved and their jobs became regular, comparatively few of them settled down locally. They were content to add a couple of hours to each working day plus the travelling expenses. I often thought that this was a tribute which their dismal looking town didn't merit, but I changed my mind when I got to know more of its streets of little terraced homes. There was warmth and protection and humanity in them.

Through the years I got to know hundreds of Wiganers, and I liked them too, they were good men, completely working class and entirely without edge or bounce.

By 1936 we were busy again, the melting shop once more was bright, lively, hot, and noisy. The dole queue was finished for me. I had quit it before work even became steady, that was a little treat I gave myself. We have moved into another house, a semi-detached, and actually our first venture away from tenements and terraced houses. We liked it so well that eventually I bought it. The hard way of course, with a deposit and a mortgage. To think that I could afford a deposit delighted me. I could hardly credit my good sense, for I was a spending man with a foolish belief in luck.

Our eldest girl Josephine was born not long before we moved house, and her sister Bernadette was born twenty months later in January 1938. By then I was forty years old and still a second-hand steel melter, and still a fit man despite frequent physical exhaustion. My wife Aileen was well and well pleased with everything around her. She sensibly accepted the fact that Josephine was mentally retarded and she lost little time in fits of wounded vanity or depression. Neither did I, we both got on with the business of putting up with it, and doing our best. We soon found there were vast compensations, there still are.

I was on one of the new furnaces, the big capacity ones that were capable of thirteen and fourteen charges per week, which meant between thirteen and fourteen hundred tons of steel. On a good week my wages were over ten pounds. This increased later on when steel prices went up and our sliding scale rose accordingly. In actual fact our wages in the heavy steel trade in 1936 had only increased 3½ per cent since 1929.

1937 was a very good year for all of us in the steel trade, especially since holidays with pay became an active fact. That we should at last get paid holidays was a great boost to our self respect. I know I went for two holidays in 1938, in Whit Week to Lourdes in the South of France, on a pilgrimage, and later on with my wife and two children to the Rosses in Co. Donegal, Bernadette being only eight months old at the time.

When I asked Bert Leadbetter for time off for the second holiday he agreed cheerfully, saying, 'After all there mustn't have been much fun on the first one.' The first one in fact had been plenty of fun, with a lovely and lively Italian girl delighting us all. Later on I showed her photograph to Bert Leadbetter and he said, 'Lovely kid. Is she married?' I answered, 'No, she has entered a convent to become a nun.' He shook his head sadly and said, 'Too bad. The poor girl had a kink.'

Natalina Di Chiacco would have laughed very heartily at Bert's woebegone opinion. She became a nun and died with other nuns when their convent in Italy was bombed in the second world war.

The new furnaces on the melting shop did nothing to improve our working conditions, although technically they were an advance on our older and smaller type. Like the rest they were basic open-hearth, with the same facility for reducing the phosphorus in the metal. I always thought the term open-hearth was a misnomer, for all furnaces of that kind have roofs and linings.

To be really advantageous we melters needed furnaces which would not require long and arduous fettling after tapping. That was our bogey; where we could create a charge into good steel in seven or eight hours, it often took as long again to repair the bottom and banks of the furnace after it.

The first-hand melters were often to blame for this, the furnace temperature being too high through faulty flame control. The excessive heat made the silica brick in the roof and linings become liquid on the surface and drip into the bath. The silica, being an acid, soon cut into the slag, and the slag, seeking resuscitation, cut into the limey dolomite banks.

The management rarely complained, they regarded this as the level of steelmaking at the time; besides, they too were sometimes at fault. It was their business to skilfully blend the steel scrap, the hot iron, and the oxides, according to the chemical analysis required in the finished steel. They didn't always do it, and sometimes circumstances made it impossible to do so. The result was that the melting sample, which was the first stage in refining, would be chock full of phosphorus, sulphur, and carbon. So much so that the melter might wonder if his charge was composed of old boots. Only the highest skill and nerve could turn such stuff into steel at all. That the skill wasn't lacking was evident, for the company was catholic in its products. Rails, sections, joists, tubes, rounds, billets, wire rods, we made the lot. This too with the minimum of instrumentation. All we had was the draught-recording-clock plus the first-hand melter's experienced eyes.

The long periods of furnace fettling was eased somewhat when an assistant manager introduced us to the wooden rabble. This was a block of hard slow-burning wood with a hole one inch diameter in the centre, through which an iron rod twenty feet long was firmly pegged. Its function was to splash out any liquid which remained in holes in the furnace baths after tapping. Each rabble was vigorously applied by a team of three melters and had a lifetime of three minutes. The rod was then withdrawn and another team operated the next rabble.

The process continued until the liquid was clear of the furnace and the melters then repaired the faults with dolomite.

Previous to the wooden rabbles we had used iron ones which were six times less effective, and accumulated metal so that often it needed six men to pull each one out of the furnace.

Lots of these prolonged fettling sorties, or 'bad bottoms' as they were always termed, could have been finished in a tenth of the time. They were a throwback to more primitive steelmaking, to the sixties and seventies of the nineteenth century, when Siemen's open-hearths really got down to their terrific part in the industrial revolution. Then furnacemen had nothing else but trouble, they were up to their necks in it learning the new routine.

The consequence was that trouble on steel furnaces became a sort of custom and practice affair. It had been going on so long that some steelmen almost believed it necessary. Like adding chromium to make stainless steel, they threw in physical exhaustion to make it good steel. The one thing to really disconcert them was a charge to 'come ready in its stocking feet', a la Billy Lane style. Then they hoped the management wouldn't notice that everything had been so easy. They also wondered if they should hand back their pay packets, it just didn't seem right to take the money.

In spite of these almost inherent inhibitions, there were many improvements in working conditions between the two world wars. Most of them were introduced by the management in the interest of increased production; some were just a banishment of bad old ways when it was realised at last that they impeded production. On the smaller furnaces we had always shovelled in iron oxides when it was necessary to boil impurities from the metal within. On the big furnaces we followed the same practice, because the first-hands were afraid to change it. My heart used to sink when I dived my shovel into a heap of iron ore that seemed mountains high. It was very hard work with very slow results. So the order went, 'Box feed the furnaces wherever possible.'

That meant the hand feeding went out, and the charging machine feeding of furnaces came in. This covered the feeding of pig iron too, for it had been our practice, in low carbon charges, to throw sticks of pig iron on the door sillplates, let them heat to almost liquid stage, and then ram them into the furnace with firehooks.

By this means the carbon in the metal was raised, which prolonged the boil, preserved the temperature, and allowed impurities to decrease.

The new method of box feeding chilled the metal when the pig iron first entered the furnace, but it soon recovered to attain the objective more rapidly. Another method, and swiftest way of all, was to pour in a few tons of hot liquid iron direct from the mixer furnace, whenever it was available.

The third-hand melters especially were glad when the management banished the heating of manganese to red-hot, before adding it to ladle when the steel was tapping. It had to be hastily shovelled from the furnace sillplate into a barrow and rushed to the rear side for the other melters to shovel it in. At each returning barrowful the third-hand was besieged by the fear of being too late and spoiling the final chemical analysis of the charge. It was akin to wheeling a barrowload of fire across a narrow plank with all hell below waiting for him to slip.

Third-hands too were glad, and so were many more, to use the pneumatic-tyred wheelbarrows in place of the old metal wheel type.

Maybe our most significant aid to production and working conditions was the water-cooled furnace. The water coursed through narrow pipes built into the brickwork of the most vital parts. It was especially useful in the gas ports. These ports, built inside each end of the furnace, were vulnerable, and it was extremely important that the gas flame entering them had a clear way. When portions of the brickwork fell down the flame was diverted to the roof and linings. This could shorten the working lifetime of the furnace, and at its worst could cause it to collapse completely. The condition of the gasports was the furnaceman's chief anxiety. It remained an anxiety as long as the furnaces were gas-flamed, but the water-cooled ports did a lot to alleviate it. In fact the water-cooling was so important that it is hard to imagine how steelmakers managed previously without it.

A very great relief too was the disappearance of the hand-propelled furnace doors. The doors remained the same type, they were heavy affairs made of firebricks, and cased in metal, cast from our own foundries. First hydraulics, and later on electricity, replaced the grim hauling and pushing to raise and lower them.

This was very good indeed, but along came some genius to improve on it. Heaven knows who he was, but I hope he's in heaven now. All he advised was to cut a spyhole through each furnace door, say the size of a dinner plate. It couldn't have been simpler or more effective. It helped the melter to view his charge, and without feeling the heat. It made drawing metal samples an easy matter instead of a tricky little business. Most important of all, it protected the melters when they used the long iron rods to clear the taphole of obstructions when tapping. Hitherto this had always been a feat of endurance, much suffering for indifferent results. Yet previous to this simple device the full door had to be raised for every action concerning the furnace and its contents.

I never heard it mentioned, and I never thought if any one shared my opinion, but I found a great relief when the melting shop floor was changed from concrete to firebricks encased in steel channels. It did away with countless holes where a man could trip and break a limb. Concrete can stand up to most things, but melting shop floors are subject to terrific bashings, and ours was no exception.

The first time I saw pure oxygen being used on a taphole I could hardly believe my eyes. Previously, a massed group of melters had futilely endeavoured, for more than an hour, to release the steel within the furnace. I was a chargewheeler at the time, and had been recruited with other chargewheelers to lend a hand. Our hammering was of no avail; one after another the sharp pointed bars buckled against the solid wall of metal that lay between us and our objective. At last old Freddy Hall, the samplepasser, said in a voice that sounded like the last trump, 'We'll have to use the oxo, boys.'

So a flexible rubber pipe was screwed into a cylinder of oxygen, and a long slender metal lance attached to the other end of the pipe. The lance was heated, and began to burn brightly as the oxygen was gently turned on. Then it was placed in the taphole by a second-hand melter, and in a moment or two the oxygen burned the solid wall of metal into liquid, and the charge went streaming into the ladle.

'That beats hammering,' I said to the second-hand, as we lifted the oxygen gear away from the heat. 'Yes,' he answered, 'but why didn't that old crocodile permit us to use it an hour ago? He's just about slaughtered the lot of us.'

True enough, we had just about hammered ourselves into the ground, and all because a foolish foreman took a manager's order too literally. 'Go easy on the oxygen,' the melting shop manager had said, 'it costs more than hammering.'

Yes, but if oxygen had been used after the first ineffective hammering, it would have saved more than one hour of steelmaking time, during any minute of which the furnace bath could have given way. It would also have saved two extra boxes of lime which was necessary to keep the slag in condition. Added to this was half a box of pig iron, which was needed to kick some life back into a charge which had gone off the boil. All this, plus anxiety and physical exhaustion, cost a lot more than a cylinder of pure oxygen.

It has been the curse of melting shops to have cautious, never-take-a-chance men of limited vision, as samplepassers. In some melting shops they are still a curse.

17

Sickness and Accidents

Health and me became the best of friends once we left Ancoats and settled nearer the steelworks. Gone were the heavy colds, the frequent bouts of flu, and in came a period of well being that needed no medicine to sustain it, nor fads and fancies to prop it up. It lasted for years, right from my late thirties into my middle forties and covered the whole of the second world war.

In that respect I was not unusual on the melting shop, for the men of my generation, and long experience in the tougher jobs, were all healthy. The fact that they were there at all proved that, for steel was a searching thing and liked its operators to be strong like itself. There was of course the odd unexpected death, as if mortality was letting us know that we hadn't come to stay. We acceded that, for we didn't really believe that our daily eight hours diet of heat, dust, gas fumes, and noise was all that the doctor ordered. It was just that our leisurely maturity kept these things at bay, while we enjoyed the pleasure of good steelmaking and good fellowship. Later on the enemies of good health would crowd in but in the meantime who cared.

Maybe steelmaking did have an occupational disease, but I never heard it mentioned, at least not distinctly and definitely like the miner's silicosis. If I had to name one, I'd say quickly, bronchitis, and after that stomach trouble. Heart trouble and rheumatism were out; I knew very few melters who suffered from either, especially heart trouble. It seemed that taking one's heart so often to the extremes of exhaustion but served to strengthen it. It could weaken of course from the throes of chronic bronchitis, but by then a man would have long quit the melting shop. Many a time after exhausting work on tapholes, I used to totter into a breeze, and sit on cold metal channels while it refreshed me. Sometimes too it would be in the winter time. I used to say to myself, 'You'll pay for this later on,' but I never did. I was thinking of rheumatism and piles, but no, they mustn't have made a note of it, for they left me alone.

I'd say at a guess that we had as many deaths from cancer as most other trades, but I only knew four men contract diabetes and only one melter suffer from eye cataract. Yet the last was scheduled under the Workmen's Compensation Act as 'Iron and Steelworker's Eye Cataract'. With good reasons, I'm sure, in some other branch of the trade.

I knew only three men through the years to lose an eye by sparks of metal or slag. A wonderfully low figure, for sparks and splashes of molten metal and slag were everywhere. At times one's flannel shirt could be riddled with spark burns, with little inconvenience to one's body, the sweat would douce them before they harmed. There were of course serious burning accidents, not every day, nor not every year, but the most likely thing nevertheless on steel furnaces. The cause of it usually was the fierce splash of white hot liquid as a large part of a furnace roof collapsed into the charge. The roof would invariably be old and much worn, and rarely took the melters unawares. This fact very likely saved lives and prevented many more accidents.

Burning accidents frequently occurred at tapping times, and could be very serious ones. It was a second-hand melter's job to bend low over his taphole and cut out the dolomite which secured it, with a long and sharply pointed light steel bar. When this was accomplished, the next job was to release the metal by hammering up a tapping bar or burning it with oxygen. But sometimes the impatient metal inside, aggravated possibly by excessive temperature, belted out of the furnace with the first touch of the bar. If the melter ever forgot such possibilities then he was in plenty danger of his life.

However there were not many fatalities on the melting shop, though its apparent confusion might seem appallingly dangerous to a visitor. It needed experience to realise that it was an organised confusion. On other parts of the works, the blast furnaces, rolling mills, and coke ovens, the fatal accidents were as few. At no time at all had we anything approaching the dreadful toll of the coalmines. Steelmaking as I knew it was a safe trade.

Yet all insurance companies didn't agree with me, for when I insured against accident and sickness I had to be content with half the benefit offered to those in milder professions.

On the melting shop we safeguarded ourselves from financial stress by shift tontines. We paid in a shilling weekly and drew out fifteen shillings weekly when we were idle through sickness or injury. Men could join all the shift tontines, three in number, and many did so. There were rules of course, and workmen officials to see that they were applied, but the tontines were extremely human. The almost certainty that a chronic sufferer would deplete the funds never barred him from membership.

When Jack Jones, M.P., became the steelworks welfare officer he had the tontines placed on a more official basis. Four shillings weekly was deducted from the members wages, the benefits were four pounds weekly, and bonuses of five pounds after certain periods of absence. At the end of prolonged periods the benefit was reduced and finally ceased altogether.

The scheme was voluntary of course and was very successful. To draw benefit plus the national health insurance meant that one did not experience real hardship until many weeks of illness had passed.

An additional benefit for sickness and injury victims was simply known as The Collection. For many years this was a haphazard affair which depended entirely on the goodwill and good memory of kindly samaritans. But these fine qualities were negative unless allied to energy. It was no use saying, 'Poor old so-and-so must be having it rough,' and leaving it at that. It needed a resolute man to say, 'Right, let's have a pencil and paper, gimme a partner to protect me from the grumblers and growlers and off we go.'

Then the pair would go up and down the melting shop collecting from each furnace complement, a half crown from first-hands, two shillings from second-hands, one shilling and sixpence from third-hands, and a shilling each from charge-wheelers. That completed, they would go to the scrap men, and also collect from the cranemen and the pitmen, ladlemen, and slag men. That would complete the job, usually a two hours affair, then back would go the two resolutes to separate the money from the insults. For some had vigorously expounded the principle which prevented them from subscribing. There were others who would grumpily refuse without expounding anything, and the ones without principles would vanish round corners at the critical moment.

The fact that one shift of melters, pitmen, and scrap men, had collected, would inspire the other two shifts to action and the combined affair would vary from fifteen pounds to twenty-two or twenty-three pounds. It depended on the popularity of the recipient, and the energy of the collectors. If a man had a reputation for meanness, it went before him, and no one would collect for him at all. A revelation, if he cared to recognise it, that all his mean little tricks he so hoped were a secret were actually pinned up on the wall.

The men who protested, profaned, and who paid, and the ones who protested, profaned, and who didn't pay, all had a case. For one reason for starting the tontines was to banish the haphazard and often unfair collections. It wasn't right that a sick or injured man, who had always been generous, should depend on the good memory and good will of a few. A little organisation or an elimination altogether was called for.

In the end our trade union branch became sufficiently interested to allot twelve weeks' absence from work as a qualifying period, to note the qualifiers, and to appoint the collectors.

I suppose I acted as collector more than any other melter

of my time. I always felt grateful to the easy men who lightened my task cheerfully, they were in the majority. To the men who refused and with a grumble, I was always resentful, and for the dodgers I had only scorn. It seemed to me always that there was a wall between the generous man and the mean one. That the one had paid admission to a kinder, more interesting world, and that the other would never know what he was missing.

As if my interest in collections was not enough, I had to institute charity raffles as well. These were swift week-end affairs, a tanner a ticket for a small prize, and a few pounds for the recipient, and all finished on the same day.

It all started when a craneman named Shanghai Childs fell seriously ill. I knew he had little money and I liked Shanghai, I liked his type, rash, improvident and generous. So I decided to send him a pound. However I needed the pound, it was the only one I had just then. I still wished Shang to have one, so I said to myself? 'What about a raffle and get a pound that way?'

Well, every one knew Shanghai, he was a good craneman, always willing, good-tempered and obliging, and that sort are a godsend on a melting shop. Besides he owed them all money from one time or another, vaguely I considered that to be an advantage. I had no trouble at all, I sent Shang his pound that same evening.

Each week-end for the following two months I sent Shang one pound, for which he was very grateful, and which he had come to regard as a pension. On the ninth week I wondered if I should chance it once more, I'd heard rumours about Shang. He'd been seen betting a pound on a racehorse, our pound, the melting shop pound, the raffle proceeds. Things looked very shaky indeed, it looked as if Shang would be forced once more to acquire his pocket money the hard way. The first three men I approached convinced me of the errors of Shang's way, and of mine. They each took the raffle tickets and cheerfully said, 'Let's call it a free week. Tell old Shang to take the tanners from the money he owes us.'

It was the end for Shanghai, he resumed work the week after, but it wasn't the end for the raffles. I carried on with them for the next twenty years, hating them all that time. There's nothing more boring than being pestered by ticket sellers except being a ticket seller. There was always someone sick or injured and always someone to tell me about them, and not once did I dare to say no. Each time I hoped for a free week a new crop of names came along. I was a well of hope to the afflicted and an affliction to the well.

Once a local newspaper heard of my activities and stated that I collected over two hundred pounds weekly. Since the highest money I ever aimed at was five or six pounds, that needed a bit of explaining. Though I contradicted that in the following issue, the damage was only partially remedied. There were actually some fools who still believed that my personal rake-off was a neat little two hundred pounds weekly.

Since I was hooked for the selling of tickets the best way I found was to adopt a ruthlessness that my inward feelings belied. I became the complete expert in delivery and in saving my breath. Each week-end I made one swift sortie down the melting shop spraying tickets left and right as I went, pushing them in hands, in jacket pockets, dropping them on cabin tables, missing no one except the notorious grouchers; melters, bricklayers, labourers, cranemen, fitters, electricians, stocktakers, they all paid their tanners to the silent salesman.

I used to get letters, just short notes of thanks from the fellows who benefited, and I used to stuff them unopened week after week in a jacket pocket. There were about fifty collected when I decided to burn them in the furnace. I checked myself in the act, for although I knew the gist of them, it seemed uncourteous to burn them unopened. So I read them one by one, and it saddened me to note that ten of the writers were dead. Collectively they gave me a reminder of man's mortality; as they died in their turn I had scarcely noticed.

The chest sufferers were the men who walked alone. It was a sign that all was not well with them, that they couldn't keep pace with the vigorous. Unthinkingly I used to slack pace and join them, but it embarrassed them, and only later I realised the reason.

There was little anyone could do for them. No one said anything to hurt a stricken man, we just silently took over his work and added an extra hour or so of sweat to our already damp shirts. This couldn't last, for the job was too strenuous to continually shoulder another man's burden. The solution would come quickly enough, for the sick man would soon fail to turn out. Indeed he would be away so long that to some he would scarce be a memory.

When he did come back at last it was to some light labouring job, and not to the furnaces. He swept the melting shop floor or he cleaned the windows of the furnace cabins. He was still not well and never would be well, and his silence was the greatest sign that it was so. Breath was too precious to waste in combating the roar of the melting shop. His voice, hoarsened by illness, would not be heard. So he would lean on the shaft of his brush or his shovel, and between whiles he would labour a little. The fact that he was now a day labourer instead of a shift worker was helpful to health. His starting time would be eight and most likely he had been awake since five recruiting the breath to proceed. But he would cling to his place in the promotion list until long after his hopes of being a melter again had gone. When he did say the word no one would have forced him, indeed his workmates would play gravely the game of health renewed to him.

At the first sign of fog he would be missing again and for longer than ever. When the winter was over and the weather warmer he would appear again, but not to work; that was a pretence that was finished for ever. Maybe he would visit his favourite pub or sit on the forms on the road that led to the steelworks. As his mates passed to and fro he'd be glad of a word and glad when they didn't stay long. He hadn't the breath for long conversation, and fit men can be thoughtless.

Those public forms and the men who sat on them haunt my conscience at times. I saw many a good man now broken in health resting on them, and many a time I passed by with an indifferent nod. Their coughing and pausing for breath irritated me. Many of them had been men with beautiful strength which they had shared generously. Johnny Meehan was one of them and many a tough spot he had helped me out of on the furnaces. Now there he sat, an outcast from the strong, on a form he could scarcely rise from.

And Mick Bennett; once his fine muscled arms were like silk, but he died of T.B. in his early forties. I didn't even have a nod for him in the end, I blamed him for malingering and I was afraid he would scrounge drinks from me. Yet I had never known Mick to scrounge a drink in his life, but I'd known him to give plenty.

I wish I had the chance all over again to sit on those forms and talk to those men in that steelworks town, but it's too damn late.

18

First-hand Melter

The day war was declared in 1939 I was in the Rosses in Donegal, enjoying a holiday there with my wife and family. The Rosses covers a wide area of some of the wildest and most beautiful scenery in Ireland, stretching from the rock- and boulder-strewn Atlantic coastline to beyond the lonely mountains of Errigal and Muckish. It is about the farthest away from war one can get in these islands. Peace is the predominate feature of the Rosses and in Bunbeg, where we lived, it was enhanced by the pleasant sound of the Clady river on its way to the sea.

Our house was only twenty-five yards or so from the river bank, and the rocky fields of our landlord, Owen O'Donnell, went right down to it. Which was very convenient for me when I went fishing.

I never knew whether my fishing was illegal or not. The people in Bunbeg were bi-lingual, with Gaelic first and often enough English limping well behind, and they all assured me that fishing was quite free. But the descendents of Lord George Hill, a famous landowner in Donegal, held the salmon rights, and their watchers patrolled the waters keenly in season.

However, by the time I arrived the salmon had reached their spawning ground in Dunlewy Lake, and the river watchers with their field glasses had gone. So too had their mobile hut from its high vantage perch, and so had Lord George's descendants, back to their English homes. So maybe the natives were right, and the rest of the fishing was free.

Still I never can trust the Irish, I know them too well. The

Englishman tells the truth, and if it's not palatable, well that's too bad but the truth must be told. I know where I stand with them. That's not the Irish way; they hate to disturb one by telling a disappointing truth. It often only makes matters worse.

Owen O'Donnell was a widower and his four young girls and one boy were reared by his mother Margaret O'Donnell. She was a small, energetic woman, very witty, and a kindly autocrat in the home. No one, and Owen least of all, disobeyed her or questioned her word. She had been widowed at twenty-four when Owen's father died after a salmon poaching episode in the Clady river. On a pitch dark night, standing to his waist in the water, he ducked under each time they shone their lamps on him. It brought on the pneumonia of which he died.

On the day before we left for home I had a last hour on the river, just below O'Donnell's house, and Myret, as Margaret was always known, joined me. 'You are off tomorrow,' she said thoughtfully. 'I am,' I answered regretfully, 'and to a far different scene from this.' 'Why go?' she asked surprisingly, and pointed across to the Atlantic, 'Sure there's fish in the sea and taties in the field, and what more do you want? Besides, you can have the house beyant us.'

The house she mentioned was the one the O'Donnell's had recently vacated. Owen had built the new one we were living in, for like most of the Bunbeg men he was peasant and builder, and fisherman too.

There was no thought of us staying; we had a home too to go back to, and a right to take anything that was coming. I started back two nights afterwards on the furnaces and took someone's place as first-hand. I was well up the promotional ladder, and heading for the last rung. Not before time, for I was just turned forty-two years old and had spent nearly half of them as a second-hand melter. The colleagues who had worked with me so often on furnace tapholes were all first-hands by then, Jack Jones, Artie McGowan, Smudger Smith, and Big Johnny Hetherington and Mick Loftus.

They were all on the same shift as me and were working that night. At one o'clock in the morning we tapped my furnace, it was the A. furnace at the beginning of the melting shop, and the one nearest the night outside. It was streaming fully into the ladle, a good bright charge, and I was well pleased by the way I had managed it. The white flame was glowing away up to the roof and lighting the night outside, when right in the middle of it the air raid sirens sounded.

It was a false warning, or a practice warning, but it was real enough to all of us that night. Actually there were many months of a phoney war between us and the real air raids, but we didn't know that. Since it was a most extraordinary time, the management were doing a night and day affair, and the two on the melting shop nearly went crazy. They were afraid that the lit-up sky would attract the whole German air force. I shared their fear and so did plenty more.

One of them actually shouted to my second-hand, a big fellow named Jack Standbank, to stop the stream and shut up the taphole straight away. Jack goggled at such an order, 'How the hell can I do that?' he demanded, 'I might as well try to stop the tide from coming in.' It was true too, and even if we could have stopped the stream of metal, the glow would have remained in the sky for some time.

We were to learn a lot more on how to behave during air raids, and when the warnings sounded we used to rush to black out every crack of light from the furnaces. After that I used to sit in the dark by the furnace side and wonder how far the metal would splash if a bomb hit it.

No bomb ever did hit them, but we had an air raid all to ourselves, for one evening getting on towards midnight a lone raider swooped down and dropped a stick of eight bombs all over the works. By extraordinary good fortune the only damage was a burnt wagon sheet and we douced it before it reached the wagon.

We were on the fringe of the Manchester air raids most of the time and very little happened to our district. Our chief bogy first of all was the blackout, and the old roof of a thousand holes had to be replaced by a fine new one. Sides were built at each end of the melting shop, and across beyond the gas producers a complete long wall of steel girders and metal sheets was erected. At each end huge metal doors opened and shut to let the locomotives bring up supplies, and to draw away the empty wagons.

Once the doors were shut in the night-time the bright lights from furnaces tapping were shut in too. That is if the warnings sounded while the steel happened to be running out. Otherwise we clayed up every crack of light as usual and remained in darkness, waiting for the all clear. The long blackouts created a new technique, for the flame still operated inside the clayed up furnaces, and it became an extra skill to control the temperature from memory. The aim was to progress the furnaces steadily so that little steelmaking time had been lost. Sometimes we managed it, and once we carried so much excess temperature that the charge broke through the furnace bottom. I was taking many first-hand shifts by then and at times I erred in the other direction, I kept the furnace temperature too low. One particular time I had a charge in beautiful condition and ready to tap when the air raid warnings sounded. Hours later when the all clear sounded my furnace was almost black out and the charge inside it a liquid no longer. I had erred, and badly.

Bert Leadbetter was far from pleased, 'I'll tell you what, Paddy,' he said thoughtfully and nastily, and before my mates on the furnace, 'you'd be better to revert back to your second-hand job and bloody well stay there.' Inside me I had the same thought but I wasn't telling him that. Instead I answered thoughtfully and nastily, 'I'll tell you what Bert, I'll see you in hell before I do that.' He said no more; he had the sense to see that he was living in a changed world, and that one of the changed things was me.

The blackout not only kept the bright lights in but it kept the dust and the gas fumes in too. It had been thrown up in panicky haste and with no regard for ventilation, or the welfare of the workmen. Many times we worked in a grey haze which was sometimes thick enough to blot out the furnace next to us. We were all in it, furnacemen, pitmen, scrapmen, cranemen, and all the maintenance trades, and it ruined many a chest before it increasingly improved.

In spite of it the general health on the melting shop was good. Men were being prosecuted for being absent from urgent munition work but it never happened where we were. We plodded along doing the best we could, and taking rather a pride in it. That seemed to be the way with most grown civilians. It was like a general front and we felt much in common with the men in the forces. There was good temper everywhere, and that despite a common and ever-present weariness. I spoke to people who, pre-war, had passed me by for years. There was nothing like the whiz of falling shrapnel for saying, 'Have you people been introduced, then let me ...'

I can't remember lacking any food. The rationing must have been devised with great skill, what we did get was better than too much. We were short on luxuries, and the most commonplace things became luxuries. I remember a sad young fellow doing a charge-wheeling shift on my furnace. His child, a girl seven years old, had recently died, and as she lay ill she had longed for an orange. 'It wouldn't have saved her life,' he told me, 'it was nothing like that, but I just wanted an orange above anything else in the world.' But there was no orange for the dying child in all the big town of Warrington, where they lived.

One welcome thing we melters never lacked was strong sweet tea, the most strengthening thing there is for revivals from hot exhausting labour. The government granted extra rations to our type of workers, and it couldn't have done a wiser thing in the pursuit of good steel.

The times, and the government's urgent invitation, made me an allotment holder. Good fresh vegetables were terrifically important then. I became an enthusiast and remained one ever since. You can't beat a vegetable allotment for a retirement hobby. Yet I've known the same hobby help kill some retired men. They were the sedentary type, little used to manual effort, and didn't realise the danger of starting it so late in life.

In between steelmaking and vegetable growing I was also a fire-watcher and a Home Guard. It intrigued me to wear a uniform at forty-odd years of age. I might have made a soldier thirty years previously, but not after a quarter century on steel furnaces. Like everything else about me I didn't go forward, nor, once approached, did I try to escape. Other steel melters in my age group successfully evaded it, but I didn't bother trying. In that respect at least I went voluntary.

Actually I was a conscript private in the Home Guards and that's what I remained to the end of my service. Other men might strain for promotion, and some of them did to the point of extinction; they killed themselves as surely as a German bullet would have done it. But I had only one ambition and that was to be an ex-conscript private of the Home Guards.

However I kept that strictly to myself and plodded along silently and often somewhat bewildered. If ever I'd gone to war I would have needed my wife with me; I never managed to adjust my uniform, with its various trappings, without her aid. Even she erred, and I bitterly reproached her for turning me out with my puttees on the wrong way. I'd been in the service for months and hadn't realised there was a right leg puttee and a left leg one.

My efforts were very up and down on the rifle range. Once my sergeant praised me for five near bull's eyes. The very next time my target sheet was completely blank, and my neighbours on each side of me had come out very well with my unexpected aid.

Sometimes when manoeuvres had me crawling through hedges and ditches all the night long, I wondered how I would survive the hours on the furnace, but I always managed. Having only an eight-hours stretch was a great help, for I always had a rest after it before going on to something else.

We did adopt an emergency continual working system, but it ceased when production decreased instead of increased. During it the cranes, through lack of maintenance time, often broke down for very long periods, and the strain on the melters made extra production an impossibility.

In February 1941 I at last became a regular first-hand melter. My rise in status meant me crossing over from Bert Leadbetter's shift to Alick Southall's shift. He was a different type altogether from Bert, and it was worth untold money for the peace of mind it gave me. He was a quiet professional as good a man as ever made steel in all the world, and his criticism, when adverse, was for one's private ear alone. That above all else made me respect him for ever. Only his praise was public, and when he thought it could do a fellow good then his voice was loud.

As a consequence all melters under Alick were content, the first-hands especially, for his character gave them confidence, and that was nine-tenths of their job.

I was very anxious to do well on the first day I took over. The furnace was charged and nearly ready to begin the refining stage, and the order was for shell steel. That meant I aimed at a final chemical analysis of between thirty and forty points of carbon, and a low sulphur and phosphorus. The other elements in the metal, the silicon and the manganese, I could depend on to look after themselves.

I'd examined the furnace thoroughly before my mate, the previous first-hand, had left for home. Since he was a regular on it, he had given me some very useful advice, for steel furnaces, like human beings, develop little idiosyncrasies. When he'd gone I lowered the furnace door, and sat down to have a word with my new colleagues.

As we talked, the charge inside the furnace lifted, and the flame rushed through the bottom and sides of all five doors. It was nothing very alarming, just as if the last solid scrap had turned over inside and dissolved in the rest of the liquid.

I raised the middle door and as I expected the slag inside was thick from end to end. 'It's time she had the medicine,' said Billy Hulme, my second-hand, cheerfully. He picked up the long-shafted sample spoon, dipped it through the spy-hole, as I lowered the door again, and poured the contents on the floor. We both examined it. 'There's sixty carbon in it,' he said, as he shook the greyish slag from the shank of the spoon, 'and there's sulphur aplenty too.'

'What would you do?' I said to Bill, well knowing his answer. He grinned and replied, 'Give her the spar. A little spar, a little lime, a little heat, a little time, and there you are.'

'Let's first give the lab. a sample,' I said, 'just to prove we have nothing up our sleeves.' So we did that, and then we gave her the fluorspar, shovelling it all over the slag, and lowered the door to let the hot gas flame do its work. Soon afterwards Harry Toal my third-hand, who was known for no reason at all as Flash Harry, came back from the lab. with our metal analysis. It showed sixty-three points of carbon, a point twelve sulphur, twenty-five points phos-phorus, and the manganese sitting pretty at thirty-five points.

'Our way', said Bill, 'is as clear as daylight. We go after the sulphur and the rest will follow it home.' We gazed in the furnace again; the fluorspar had thinned the slag, and was making it contact the liquid metal underneath it. The charge was beginning to boil, and in that boil lay our hope of the sulphur diminishing. Whether the rest of the elements fol-lowed it home remained to be proved. For the present, to concentrate on sulphur was enough, for it is often a wayward puzzling element in steelmaking.

'We'll let her boil freely,' I said, 'then we'll add lime, a box, maybe two boxes, and maybe more spar to help it flux quicker.' We lowered the door, and Bill, dipping the sample spoon through the spyhole, poured some metal on the floor. 'What do you think, Flash?' I asked Harry. The third-hand answered, 'she may be just fifty points of carbon, no more than that.' He flaked the rapidly darkening slag from the spoon shank with his nailed boot. It fell easily on the floor, and it

G

was less grey in colour, more a dull black than the previous time. 'The sulphur's going', he announced, 'and so is the phosphorus. She'll be ready for the pot in one hour from now.'

Brave words from Flash Harry. I hoped he would be right, but we needed a 0·04 per cent sulphur, and that was a long drop from twelve points. I took the lime and the time and the heat and the spar again, and we didn't sample again until the slag was in condition. That meant just enough iron in it to hold the sulphur, and not too much iron, lest the sulphur went back into the metal.

'What did I tell you?' said Flash later on, as he handed me the next sample result. The sulphur and phosphorus both were a straight up 0·05 per cent, the carbon was 0·35, and the manganese was 0·21 per cent. Bill Hulme drew another sample and Flash Harry prepared to take it to the laboratory, as Alick Southall came along.

'We have a jeenyus here,' said Bill, nodding at me. 'How much did you pay for his transfer, Alick?' asked Flash Harry. Southall grinned, gazed in the furnace and said, 'she's in lovely condition, Paddy. Give her one more box of lime to hold the carbon, while Bill opens the taphole.' Ten minutes afterwards the sample result justified his confidence; as Billy Hulme put it, 'she was one for the pot.' As I watched the steel flow from the furnace into the ladle, I felt that mine was a dream debut.

19

Instrumentation

My father died in 1943 and I think he was glad that his time had come. He was a quiet man always and a lonely one after my mother died. But loneliness suited him. He was never in dread of it, and it never made him an object of pity like it does to some old men. He remained too strong and vigorous for that to happen to him. People liked him and respected him, and I think from the way they spoke of his death that his peacefulness had helped them. I could understand that, for it helped me too, and it still does. Other men have affected me like that and some of them too were in my father's position, they were widowers after happily married lifetimes and then just marking time, just peacefully waiting.

My father was only three days ill when he died of pneumonia, and it seemed a fitting end. It is often the strong man's way to die.

When the war ended the big thought in my mind was what would happen to our trade. For I remembered what happened after the first war and so did the rest of the senior melters. Some tried to tell the younger ones about it, but they were wasting their time. The young fellows listened for a few minutes in polite silence to this piece of working-class history, and then resumed the fascinating present. They had their cars and their house mortgages to talk about, and that was more important than listening to gnarled old doomsters whose bodies were shaped to their toilsome pasts.

Jack Jones had left us, he had become M.P. for Bolton in the Labour government of 1945. He went off to help steel nationalisation come true, and in the enthusiasm of the great labour landslide we hoped on the melting shop that it would come soon. With the wartime controls on and a government that would keep them so we felt that the spadework was done. We had five or more prosperous post-war years behind us by the time nationalisation did happen, and we had lost our enthusiasm for it. So much so that we hardly noticed it arrive and we hardly noticed when it went out a few months afterwards.

I was earning about seventeen pounds a week then and second-hands and third-hands were earning up to fourteen and twelve pounds weekly when their furnaces were producing well. Each year the government was setting us an output target and each year we were exceeding it. To make sure that we would continue to do so we adopted the continuous working week system.

This didn't increase our working hours but it curtailed our traditional week-end break. Instead of it we only had one week-end out of every seven, the rest of our weekly breaks occurring on weekdays. We missed those week-ends when we were free like other workers. There is something apart, something lonely and disturbing about making steel while the rest of the world plays, and the feeling persists.

Otherwise we had little to grumble about, for the system was eminently sensible. It reduced overheads, it produced more steel, it increased our wages, and it advanced a great deal of promotion. It was a national affair of course and was really a throwback from the bad old times. It had been agreed between masters and our trade union years ago to do this very thing. The one drawback at the time to put it in action was a fearful lack of prosperity.

When we were awarded the forty-two hours week a few years afterwards, from then onwards the rest periods really meant something. There's plenty to like about a two-days midweek break; shopping is easier and cheaper, so is entertainment, so is travel, and best of all it's peaceful.

Although top wages on the furnaces were good, that was little consolation to the men at the other end, and the job held less attraction than formerly. Young fellows could pick and choose, there were more jobs than men. They came and stayed long enough to earn a few pay packets, and then went off to something else. But there were others among them who gradually succumbed to the interest that is always in steel-making, and stayed.

In a way it's a grand thing to be used only to prosperity, and the staying newcomers took every improvement in steel-making as their natural right, and asked confidently for more. Whereas we who had spent our youth in bad times were always a little surprised as well as gratified about improved conditions. Many of us had a certain inward humbleness about it all.

I know I welcomed two good canteens, and a modern first-aid station with a doctor and a nurse attending daily. I was very glad too to be able to shower and change before leaving the works. That has certainly sent the old style of steelworker into oblivion. One would be hard put to tell a young steelworker's profession as he walks off the job today. The melters of long ago in their heavy boots and white sweat towels, carrying teacans and metal lunchboxes, would goggle at the good suits and silk shirts of the moderns. If they carry anything, it will be a transistor.

Sometimes they go too far. One, a chargewheeler with me, a returned soldier named Arthur Kinsey, wouldn't work without what he called protective clothing. This meant a very thick cream-coloured duffle coat with hood attached. They were remarkably useful for keeping extreme heat out, as well as keeping the cold out. In fact they were good common sense, which is possibly one reason why I never wore one.

At the time we were on a furnace at the end of the melting shop where some rain was blowing in, and Arthur wanted protection from it. He had a ten minutes' job to perform, shovelling a barrow load of steel scrap turnings. I thought his anxiety peculiar, seeing how he must have braved something more dangerous than a little rain, shot and shell for example. After all I had braved falling shrapnel myself, and I was no hero. But Arthur got his duffle coat all right and no trouble at all, and a steel helmet too, so he was prepared against hailstones as well. I used to hope he would put the hood of the duffle coat over his steel helmet, but he never did.

Though there was one time when he entered the first-aid station in great distress. He complained of a dreadful buzzing in his head. The chap in charge didn't examine Arthur, he examined his steel helmet instead, and found a cricket in the lining.

One by one, without upheaval or loss of work, our furnaces changed from gas-flamed to fuel-oil-flamed. It was the start of our instrumentation, for every furnace bore clocks denoting the gallons of oil and the poundage of steam being used. The gas producers running alongside the melting shop became obsolete, so did the wisps and clouds of black gas throughout the melting shop. It was a lot cleaner process and a lot noisier, for the oil was injected into the furnaces by steam atomisation.

It didn't make a great difference to our steelmaking, or cause any great study of new methods on the melters' part. We all went forward from gas to oil quite naturally. One thing it did do was to relieve us of the gasports, and all the work and the anxiety attached to them, and that really was something. It altered the construction of the furnaces somewhat; where previously gas and air were heated by the regenerators before mixing in the furnaces, now only the air was heated.

With the introduction of instrumentation the hit or miss element in steelmaking was greatly reduced. In its place came a uniformity of production and at far less cost in raw materials. Of equal importance to me and my kind was the diminishing wear and tear on the human body and mind. I never really knew how bad a steel melter I was until the temperature clocks told me. The information might have shattered me only for the long founded suspicions which intermittently assailed me. Sometimes I was up in the clouds and sometimes I secretly wondered why the firm paid me at all.

For years I never knew the exact temperatures of my steel-making, nor did I know the safe temperatures for making it. First of all I had to be sure that these aids were not taking my job away from me. I didn't want to be just a furnace tender doing an odd uninteresting chore while infallible instruments made perfect steel. That wasn't the way of it at all; steel melters were still needed and the instruments, though reliable, were not infallible. It was still necessary to have men who knew what was going on in steel furnaces.

Where once I adjusted my stack damper by hand I now touched a button on the controls panel. With the same ease I controlled the fuel and air supply, and the waste coke-oven gases. I could set my roof temperature at the point desired and reverse my fuel and air immediately. I could tell at a glance if the regenerator heat balanced, and determine the air supply necessary to effect lightning combustion in the furnace bath.

There was one instrument which was my especial favourite. It was a mobile one which an operator trundled from furnace to furnace and which we all knew as The Dipper. It recorded the temperatures of all the furnaces at varying stages in the refining processes. The Dipper was an expressive name considering that the operator projected it into the slag and metal, but Oracle was a better name still. One had but to take heed of the instrument's recordings to be on the right lines for good safe steelmaking. It put courage in the over-cautious melters and it restrained the impetuous ones. The sample-passers welcomed it most of all, for with its recordings ascertaining the tapping temperatures, about 50 per cent of their responsibility was wiped out.

I always had a feeling of inadequacy when I took charge of a furnace after its general overhaul. The feeling increased as I grew older and the furnaces magnified in proficiency and in cost. Everything would be new and thousands upon thousands spent on it. Scores of men would have swarmed over it and laboured to bring it to perfection. For three weeks, night and day, the bricklayers would have built and their helpers carried; the electricians would have replaced old gear everywhere for new; the fitters would have perfected everything mechanical, and the last coat of aluminium paint would have been applied. Then I would go along to take over. Tough, gnarled, heat-worn, yet heat-resistant like a used silica brick, I should have been vibrant, modern and versed in technicology as well as practicality. For all that I would wrestle and strain and coax and worry oceans of steel from it. Steel that would go out to the world in thousands of ways, and all of them solid. I wouldn't be thinking of that, for steel to me was a white-hot liquid bubbling in a furnace bath, and never a solid at all.

There were young fellows around me who studied the technology of steelmaking but I never had much patience with them, they were all technology and no manuality. Since they knew nothing at all about practical steelmaking, I resented them trying 'to tell me'. They leaned on the shovels they hated to use and complained bitterly that I 'wouldn't be told'.

I was making steel before they were born, but I thought little of that, for in my case it was more repetitive than progressive; still, it was enough of a reason for me to be doing the telling.

I had to do the telling in plenty to the students in metallurgy who used to spend their holidays on the melting shop. They pursued practicality with zest, and some worked in front of the furnace so much that I wondered if they would ever lose their furnaceman's burnt complexions again. They also developed furnaceman's thirsts for themselves, and being open-handed chaps they further developed the already developed thirsts of some of the regulars. I hope they learned plenty; it was a pleasure to meet them and a pleasure to tell them.

I rarely knew a furnaceman who wasn't willing to answer any question truthfully on steelmaking. But I knew plenty, they were nearly all first-hands, who were almost inarticulate about the job in which they were experts. None of them were quite so bad as the melter I saw portrayed on an outside television programme a few years ago. An interviewer asked him, 'What is steel?' and the man in charge of a modern furnace hesitated, then answered, 'I don't know. You must ask the foreman.'

Smudger Smith, a strip of a man who never weighed more than eight stones in his life, and the best first-hand melter I ever knew, was always embarrassed by questions. 'Watch me,' he used to say uneasily, 'and keep on watching me all the time and you may pick it up.' He couldn't explain how he removed the sulphur element from the metal so handily. Or how he controlled the temperature so effectively and safely. Smudger had never heard of the modern term, 'slag control': he called it 'working a charge' and he was a complete steel-maker, a natural.

The future will see all melters well versed in technology as well as practicality. That is if the basic open-hearth process is not replaced entirely by the tonnage oxygen process. I know nothing about the latter but if it, or some even more advanced method makes steelmaking too easy and certain, then the melter may not be so important or his job so interesting. The fascinating thing about the basic open-hearth is the personal skills involved in its steelmaking. In the past especially it gave scope for tremendous satisfactions even when physical exhaustion was plentiful. Instrumentation and progress in furnace building have bettered conditions and since that is so and the old skills are still necessary it is an even more interesting job as a result, and the melters of today with their fair educational background, should make the best of both worlds. The concerns they work for are vast and powerful, and dead keen to further sound education in technology.

If I had a wish at all in steelmaking, it would be to see a library inside each Works, as centrally situated as the work's canteen, and used as frequently. There would be study classes in it, and besides books on technology, there would be histories of the iron and steel trade in Great Britain. The histories of course would include the activities of the steel masters' federation, and the steelworkers' confederation. There would be a museum too with exhibits of all the step by step developments in the trade, and albums with personal histories not only of management, but of workers too. The head of my own firm, for instance, was a tremendously interesting man named Sir John James, and his personality was matched on the melting shop by men like Jack Jones. All this would help goodwill between masters and men.

Unlike the American steel history in Carnegie's day, there is no Homestead massacre in British steel to remember with bitterness. True, the masters gave little away, but there has been give and take on both sides and admiration at times. All this is a good enough base to build contentment, and pride in one's job, and loyalty.

But in the great amalgamations of today just who can the steel melters be loyal to? Not to the shareholders surely, or to the top brass in management? For those are all people they've never known or ever will know. The highest level of management the furnacemen know are the melting shop managers, and when they are good the men know it. A good melting shop manager who is keen and knowledgeable on his job and fair in dealing with the men can set a tremendous example. If he is an honest man he can make men glad they are steel furnacemen. But if he is one of the kind who assign workmen to clean his car, dig his garden, and even do his wife's housework, and all on the firm's time and money, then he is a bad example. He is not only a thief but he is a creator of thieves, and of disloyalty. I've seen both sorts.

20

Holidays

By 1952 my wages averaged £18 weekly and I was still fit to earn them and to spend them too. Each year my wife said, 'You promised to take us to Rome,' and each time I answered 'All right then we'll go to Rome.' I was always in earnest, for it was the place above all that I wanted to see. But every time she would say, 'We can't afford it, we will go next year.'

We always winded up by going to the Rosses in Donegal, and continued to do so until Margaret O'Donnell died. After that the girls got married and the home broke up and Owen O'Donnell went to live with one of them in Glasgow. Their two houses still stand near the Clady River with the windows and doors boarded, silent and lonely like so many more in the Irish countryside.

My daughter Bernadette was fifteen and pursuing her education in a convent grammar school in Manchester. Josephine was seventeen and had been pursued by her education in the local Catholic school. Poor Jo, it never caught up with her. I was in doubt about sending her to the school at first, and whether she would be accepted, but there was no opposition: she was taken in as readily as the clever ones.

The headmaster, Mr Havekin, was a fine teacher and even more important to Jo and us, he was a wise and kindly man. His staff took after him, so Jo was happy enough. She always had champions among her classmates to guard and fight for her against the jeers of the thoughtless. I still meet them, they're grown up women now, married, and with children of their own at school and I still feel grateful to them.

In 1953 my wife uttered her usual statement on Rome, then made her usual decision, and compromised for Crolly village at the foot of the Crolly mountain in Donegal, and within sight of the trout-laden Crolly river. The village was a few miles from Margaret O'Donnell's old home in Bunbeg, and the small hotel we stayed in was full literally to the rafters. That meant four other guests besides us.

The hotel owner was an old man and extremely lively and entertaining. His fare was excellent and his charge so moderate that it made me wonder if he'd heard of the second world war, or even the first one.

I had two ambitions to fulfil in Donegal that year, first to undergo the penitential pilgrimage in Lough Derg, and second to go to Glenties, where Patrick McGill the Navvy Poet was born.

The pilgrimage was an old established feature of Catholic life in Ireland, from the time of St Patrick himself, more than fifteen hundred years ago. I travelled the fifty miles journey to the island in a big American car owned and driven by a man named Maurice, and with six local people who were strangers to me. We reached the lonely and quite stormy waters of Lough Derg in the early afternoon, and crossed over to Station Island in a large and crowded motor boat.

As we neared the island I had a great longing to be travelling in the opposite direction, for I had a fierce headache and I well knew the reason of it. It was hunger, for in compliance to the pilgrimage rules I had fasted from the midnight previous. It was also apprehension of what was to follow. My fast on that day would only be broken once by a meal of dry bread and black tea. I would enjoy, or suffer, the same solitary meal on the second and third day of the pilgrimage, and in between there were all sorts of prayerful tortuous practices to be observed. I told myself dolefully that I was a devil for punishment.

The island was small and packed with four buildings which ran down almost to the water edge, St Patrick's Basilica, the chapel of ease, and the male and female hostels. In between were narrow paths along which were prayer stations, at each of which the barefooted pilgrims paused and prayed. Some of these stations were the beds of ancient saints, and were just sharp pointed rocks jutting from the earth. They were extremely painful to feet used to leather and to city pavements.

Some hundreds of us thronged into the Basilica to pray and keep vigil, all through the first night. The second day was a replica of the first, and in it weariness and lack of sleep impinged on everything I did. The Basilica walls seemed to shake as I gazed on them, and my hunger was entirely submerged by the thought of the dismal fare.

Yet I was far from unhappy, and looked forward with great anticipation to my hostel bed. Never for years did I experience such sweet sleep, my head hit the pillow at nine o'clock and two minutes later, at six o'clock the next morning I was facing the last of the penitential days. We left the island at midday, it was bright and sunny, and as I looked back at the Basilica from the crowded boat I had a feeling of exhilaration and health which I wouldn't have swopped for a million dollars.

The following day I set off to Glenties and in a hired car, but not with Maurice driving. Since no penitential exercises were included, my wife and the girls were pleased to come along. I had no idea what I should meet at Glenties for I hadn't heard or read a thing about McGill for many years. If he was alive I reckoned then that he would be about sixty-six years old, that was still young enough for him to be back in Glenties and 'mowing Irish meadows'. For that was the hobby listed under his name in an old copy of *Who's Who*. The *Manchester Guardian* had quoted it to me when I wrote seeking knowledge of McGill's whereabouts.

The quotation had given me hope, for where, I asked myself, would he mow Irish meadows except back home. I had read all his novels on navvy life and crude stuff it was too, and not likely to please his own folk. I knew that he left the navvy life to join the editorial staff of a London newspaper, and that he served as a stretcher-bearer in the Royal Irish Rifles throughout the first world war. I also knew that he had written two books on his war experiences and a play on the same theme. The play only lasted a fortnight on the London stage but the critics praised it. One claimed it to be better than *Journey's End*. 'A pity', he wrote, 'for McGill's sake that it dealt with the common soldier instead of the officer class.' Still watching out for McGill's progress, I read that he had an appointment in the library at Windsor Castle. The *Manchester Guardian* told me that he was copying manuscripts there under the direction of a Canon Dalton. He stayed a year or so and then resigned; that would be in 1925 or so. I read of it in a one-line newspaper report and that was the last I ever heard of him.

Glenties was a jewel of a place. It was the prettiest little town I had ever been in in Ireland, but they could tell me nothing. The meadows had been mowed but not by Patrick McGill. 'He went away', said one old man, 'when he was fourteen years old and he never came back. It was just as well, for his books were not good and there would be no welcome for him here.'

In that very Catholic part of Ireland I knew what he meant. From Glenties I went to Dungloe, another neat little town by the sea and sixteen miles away, and there I met McGill's nephew, a prosperous young business man named John Devlin. 'I'm thirty years old', he told me, 'and I've never met Patrick McGill. He went away and he stayed away. One thing I do know, that his sister, my mother, would never allow any of his books in our home.' That didn't surprise me. 'I heard', he said, 'that after he left Windsor Castle he joined up with some other writing fellows in America, married there, and became a scriptwriter in Hollywood.'

He shook his head, 'very likely he'll be dead.' Very likely indeed. But I hoped that he was still alive and that he still might mow those Irish meadows.

It was 1957 before we saw Rome, and a few other famous

places in Italy as well. Venice, Florence, Genoa, Loreto, Pisa, we spent some time in each of them during our fortnight's conducted tour, with four days and nights in Rome as the highlight of it. This time Bernadette didn't travel with us. She was a young lady twenty years of age and preferred holidays with her friends. She was still a student, and was in her fourth year at the Manchester College of Art. Josephine went with us of course, for at twenty two she was still a child, and always would be.

I loved Italy, the bright air so lovely to breathe and so lovely to live in, and so different from the gas fumes and dust of the melting shop. I puzzled over the fact that men still died in such wonderful places, and since that was true then how account for the fact that I in my atmosphere had lived at all. If I had my life to live again I would ask for twice as much toil and sweat but only to be done in the sweet fresh air. I saw the effect of the good atmosphere on one member of our party especially. He was an old man travelling alone and terribly afflicted with bronchitis. So much so that it was agony, not only for him but for the three persons who shared his table at every meal.

They were Portuguese, father, mother, and daughter of sixteen or so, and very modern and aristocratic. They were very sorry for themselves, that their holiday should be spoiled by a sick man who should not have travelled at all. There was reason in that, and I agreed with them, but in a far lower tone, for I felt the old chap had enough to bear. 'Let's swap tables with the Portuguese,' said my wife to me, as we lunched on the second day. She had noticed the disgust directed towards the old man. I didn't hesitate, and neither did the Portuguese, I think they would have paid me for the transfer.

As it was, we were well repaid, for the pure Italian air gradually vanquished the old man's ailment. He was a Scotsman named Jim Allen and a thoroughly interesting, well read man. We enjoyed each other's company immensely.

The tour was strenuous, possibly these affairs mostly are, and I suppose the comfort increases as the price increases.

Ours was moderately priced and we had no grumbles, even if we did arrive late at our hotels with time only for a late dinner, and bed, and the prospect of a 6 a.m. rising. Each morning after breakfast our party, forty strong, sleepily entered our luxury coach, and away we went to our next outpost. Being as poor a daytime sleeper in Italy as anywhere else, I used to turn round from my seat near the front, and gaze on the somnolent scene. Every one would be nodding, and immediately behind me, my wife Aileen and our little afflicted daughter would be fast asleep, Jo always with her head tucked under her mother's protecting arm. They looked so secure, so innocent, and so peaceful that always I experienced a delightful wave of happiness as I gazed on them.

I have read, and I have heard of conducted tours being condemned by superior persons. At such moments it would have been wasted time trying to convince me.

Yet there is nothing so touristic, so strange and remote from the country it travels in, as a conducted party sitting high up within its swiftly moving glass walls. The coach is a kingdom in itself with the courier as king, the driver as minister of transport, and the tourists as subjects. Outside are the wolves: the hotel-keepers, the restaurant owners, the waiters, the shopkeepers, the street vendors, all of them exploiters who scarcely bother to conceal their contempt for their victims.

I liked Florence, there was elegance in the people as well as in their wonderful city. Among other reasons I liked Rome too for the same thing. When we reached Venice I was startled into sudden delight to see reality measure up so well to a dream. The dark-complexioned gondoliers seemed tremendously romantic but I liked the workaday gondoliers better, and because they were not elegant. Their crafts were filled with merchandise, and some were filled with stones and mortar, with hardy looking well-muscled men scudding them along. It reminded me of the peasants in Keady leaving the town after a market day, and heading their loaded carts for up country. Though what up country meant to a Venetian I never found out.

At Pisa we stayed an hour or two in the brightest of bright days and in the sheerest of clear air. The white basilica gracefully fitted into the scene, and so did its campanile. I saw them first and then when I saw the tower I gasped, 'Upon my soul it does lean.' Although I had gazed on its pictures scores of times I was still amazed to see it lean so much.

A short holiday in Rome can be chaotic for persons who have travelled little and whose knowledge of history is scanty. Yet more by accident than design we managed to bring some order into our visit and to create some memories.

There were, of course, in our hearts the three concrete ambitions of all Catholics, to see the Pope, to visit the Vatican, and to hear Mass in St Peter's. In company with my wife Aileen and little Jo I achieved them all. In addition, while they were shopping in Via Cola di Rienzi, the street we lived in, I visited the tomb of St Cecilia in the Catacombs of St Calixtus. After that I went to Trastevere which is a district behind the Vatican, and I lost myself in its fascinating alleys.

On either side of them the closely packed houses looked as old as Rome itself, and all the washing of the world seemed to be hanging from the windows high up. Beneath them on street level were many small workshops, just cavities and seemingly without doors, where men joinered and soldered, and tailored. I glanced into them all and would have loved to linger, only I was doubtful what constituted bad manners in Rome.

I left Trastevere and rode on a bus which was very crowded. It was hard work getting on it for Italians don't queue, they stampede, and it was twice as hard getting off it. Nevertheless I enjoyed my proximity to the workaday citizens, and I made it my business to use the buses as much as possible. The service was the cheapest I ever rode on and the most efficient, I was even obliged to it for a busmen's strike. This was a three-hour affair from two until five one afternoon when we were returning from the Tivoli fountains. It gave us a chance to have a real good look at the great railway station which Mussolini built.

We were very content, Aileen and Jo and me, sitting there drinking coffee and watching Roman life go about its daily business. Everyone was elegantly dressed in bright light clothes which matched the lovely day. Lots of the men were incredibly handsome; they were even more noticeable to me than the women. As they streamed up from the low-level trains the tobacco kiosk near us did a brisk trade and I noticed many people buying only two cigarettes, and in fact some bought only one. This puzzled me very much, they looked like millionaires yet they bought their cigarettes like misers. I mentioned it to a little Mexican I met in our hotel that evening, 'It's bella figura,' he said, 'they were not millionaires, each man will probably be pressing the pants of his only good suit at this moment, and enjoying his sole cigarette as he does so. And as he presses and smokes his one good shirt will be drying on the window sill.' He saw my surprise and continued, 'The average workers in Rome do not make a good wage but they like to make a good show. That's bella figura.'

The Vatican museum amazed me, and in the end the countless treasures in the vast rooms and corridors bewildered me. It was thrilling to be there, to be a part of such a cosmopolitan crowd and like most of them we lingered longest in the beautiful Sistine Chapel. We were all together, our whole party, and guided by a tall old man who kept saying anxiously, 'Minda da step, minda da step.' It was good advice, for lots of the time we were gazing at the wonderful ceilings. At the end of his task and his patter completed, he said pleasantly and hopefully, 'It is my birthday today, I am seventy-four.'

I wondered how many times he had repeated this to Vatican parties, and I determined to help him. So I held my palm open showing a five hundred lire note, and said to our party meaningly, 'For the guide.' To my pleasant surprise the Portuguese family, father, mother, and beautiful young daughter each handed me a one thousand lire note. The rest, encouraged by this munificence, weighed in handsomely, and five people who looked like Germans, and who may or may not have understood, also contributed. The old guide was in no doubt about what was going on, and there was a light in his eye like the star of the sea when I handed him nearly six thousand lire. So far as he was concerned the Vatican was mine for the asking.

I enjoyed St Peter's, a glorious pile inside and out, and most of all I enjoyed it early in the mornings. Then I used to slip out before breakfast for a quiet mass and communion offered up by a priest from God knows where. There were always scores of masses being offered up by priests from all over the world. No sooner was an altar vacated then along came another vestment robed figure preceded by his acolyte. I always made for St Joseph's altar; I suppose I should have gone to St Patrick's altar with a name like mine. But St Joseph the Workman is the saint I like best and through the years I've found him to be an excellent liaison between heaven and me.

On my way back I always broke my fast with a doughnut and a capuchino at an excellent espresso in the Via Cola di Rienzi. Then, never forgetting to drop my five lire tip on the saucer, and feeling very Roman, I would saunter off to my hotel and breakfast.

On the one Sunday morning we spent in Rome we went to mass, had breakfast, and joined our party to travel to Castel Gondalpho where Pope Pius was still in his summer residence. It was beautiful countryside, the day was lovely, the crowds were great, and when we left the coach the climb was up and up and up. The congestion as we neared the great square was terrific, and I feared for old Jim Allen who was with us. But he made it, he just had to or die for there was no getting back. We were in position with forty thousand others when the frail slight figure of Pius appeared on a high-up balcony. It was midday and hear me God it was a thrill to see him and to hear him lead us in the angelus, a thrill too to hear the mighty responses. Then he blessed us all with the most practised hand in the world, and Jim Allen, Aileen and Jo and me went off to drink the local wine at a rough hewn table. We were served by a rough hewn man who had seen more sun than I ever have, or will.

On our last evening in Rome the three of us went out after dinner and sat in some small square enjoying the lovely night. I had no regrets at leaving Italy but I regretted exceedingly that I didn't come long ago when I was young. I had grown old and scarcely knew a thing about the beauty of the world. So many more I had known on the steel furnaces who had lived and died without even the stirring of a wish to see Rome. They had seen beauty in a neatly papered wall, in a well cobbled clog, in the bottom of a pint measure, and in a pot of liquid steel, and they had been good men without even knowing a thing about the beauty of the world.

The thought I carried the following morning as our coach rolled along the Via Cola di Rienzi, was not of Vatican Rome, or Ancient Rome, or the people of Modern Rome. It was of two delightful cats, mother and daughter, who sat sleek, well-fed, and contented, watching our preparations for departure with benevolent interest. They belonged to the magnificent pasticceria next door to the Hotel Joli. I remembered the young one rubbing its head happily against the mother's snow-white fur, and the tremendous serenity of the older cat as she received its attentions.

'I would love', said my wife, and with tears in her eyes, 'to come back to Rome, to see the Vatican again.' 'A good thought,' I answered, and fell silent. I was thinking how I too would love to come back to Rome, to that wonderful fish soup they serve in a restaurant in Trastevere.

21

Pneumonia

At sixty years old I found steelmaking very hard work. Not because harsh manual labour had increased, it hadn't, but because my health and strength had decreased. There was something hanging over me, a threatening, 'I can get you when I want and I'm coming soon,' sort of feeling. I could do little about it but wait and see, and in the meantime I made steel and didn't miss a day in the making of it. The fellows working with me said, 'Oh Paddy's a killer no longer, he's the easiest first-hand in the shop to work with now.' They forgot that instrumentation and general improvement in steel production had helped to make me so. I didn't bother to point that out, nor did I tell them that the old pufferoo was there no longer, that if I didn't get a fair wind I couldn't get along at all.

I was making steel all right and without much effort or worry and because of that it was the best steel I ever made. There was no situation that my vast experience couldn't cope with, and no period in my working life when I cared less what happened.

I was lonely too, not for the sight of human beings, they were all around me, but because age forces loneliness on the manual worker. I could no longer swing on or off the melting shop with the younger men at the beginning or end of the day. Their unthinking strides had me saying, 'You go ahead, boys, I'm in no hurry.' They heeded me of course and without offence soon let me always walk alone. I became a silent man because I found it a strain to talk and to hear through the noise of the steam atomisers. I was silent too because I had not much in common with the younger men. They were in the thick of the melting shop life just as I had been, now I had outgrown it and few of my generation were left.

Nothing of this protruded on my home life, it was in excellent shape, my wife was well and the same busy little woman and good neighbour. Little Jo was happy in her tiny world and was well looked after by us all, especially by her aunt Josie. Bernadette was still at her art studies and aiming for a diploma in design.

I often wondered about her and whether she had peace within herself. It wasn't easy for her to contemplate her sister it made her virtually an only child and with much of the loneliness of one. We used to talk of it, my wife and I, but there was nothing we could do except anxiously hope that she would not feel set apart by what set her sister apart. I never uttered such thoughts to her, I enjoyed her company and I was proud of her, but I was not communicative on certain subjects and not demonstrative at all. I was not the effusive, explosive, or kissing sort of a father, I was handicapped because I was the son of Irish peasants who had been handicapped because they had been the children of Irish peasants. None of us were to blame for that, and there was virtue in it as well as drawbacks. But there was little of the simple, uneducated peasant in this tall fine daughter of ours, and the words I could say to a simpler person were not the words for her.

In the February of 1958 I wasn't feeling well, but I carried on making steel until the middle of the month. Then on the fifteenth I wakened up in the thick of pneumonia. It was no influenza verging on pneumonia sort of thing, but the real humdinger, life and death, touch and go affair. 'Don't get up until Friday,' my doctor flung at me as he hurried away. He was almost buried under influenza cases at the time. 'What a hope,' I thought, 'I'll be dead before then.' His name was Donnelly and he was an Irishman. I like my doctor to be Irish; some of them are scallywags who never get over their wild student days in Dublin, but the majority are grand fellows and mine was no exception. Dr Donnelly was resolute, but so was the pneumonia, and the pair determined to give each other a run for the money. I wasn't much help, I was too ill to know which side I was on.

It took the good doctor a full week to clear all the leering demons away from my bedside. They roosted on the bedrail like buzzards, they rode round and round me on an endless belt, and they hung from the patterns of the window curtains. At the end of the first week I remembered who I was but the knowledge wasn't consistent, nor was it very heartening. When I pulled round somewhat I had plenty of visitors, tough steelmen most of them. They used to sit and talk for two hours at a stretch and set me back two days in my efforts to keep up with them. They were not what the doctor ordered and I should have ordered them out while I still had breath left. Instead I encouraged them to defy my wife's and her sister's good nursing.

'It will be months and months', said Dr Donnelly regretfully, 'before your strength returns.' I didn't believe it would ever return, I could have slipped into death as easy as wink. 'Half in love with easeful death' was very, very true for me then. Yet I'd always been afraid of death and had spent many a precious minute measuring my mortality against eternity. When I did manage downstairs for the first time the television was going and a comedian was performing. Since he had always made me sick when I was well, it looked as if he had a fair chance of finishing me off altogether. But I resisted, for there was no 'easeful death' about that fellow, and my wife switched over to a 'Relax with Michael Holliday' programme. Poor Holliday, he died tragically a few years afterwards, but that evening he did me good, I took him at his word and relaxed.

When some strength really did come back to me I went off to Conway in North Wales for a month's convalescence. The Iron & Steel Confederation have a fine place just outside the town and I went there. I enjoyed it hugely, for it was a piece of gracious living which did me much good, and I was grateful to the sensible matron and her pleasant staff. With the minimum of fuss they produced the maximum of content.

The home held about forty men, and it was nearly full each of the weeks I was there. We represented about twenty of the steelworks in Britain and we didn't look a bad lot at all in the mass.

Conway was a good place for thinking and I had plenty of it to do. I wasn't the only one, there were some very thoughtful men sitting in the bright May sunshine in the grounds of that fine home. I didn't want to go back to the furnaces, for the melting shop was no place for a man with impaired lungs. But I was four years and a bit from pension time, so it had to be done. The alternative was a dreary so-called 'light job' sweeping the melting shop floor, or cleaning a few office windows. That was not for me, for it meant a great reduction in wages; no removal from the melting shop atmosphere; a loss of prestige; and a loss too of the great creative interest which makes a steelman's life eminently bearable.

So back I went, permanently short of breath, but thankful that the old exhaustive days were far behind me. The worst periods for me were the tapping times, for then I buckled in with the rest to repair the furnace bath. I could have left it safely to the other melters but I would have revealed my weakness, and pride didn't allow me to do that. So long as I remained fit to fettle my furnace then I had a right to hold on to my job. That was the way I looked at it, but nevertheless as I swung the dolomite high from my shovel I looked out anxiously for big Frank Arstall and Irish Jackie Rea. When they came along my life was saved. They were both second-hand melters, fit, strong, and tremendously willing, prodigal with their energy and downright good fellows.

I never revealed what they meant to me and I don't think they ever suspected. If they had they would have carried me about, and that was the last thing I wanted.

Receding health, increasing years, and retirement loom-ing, was good for my savings bank. I was in earnest about it at last, for always I had been a spending man and liked to play the horses too. Now I told myself there would be four years grandstand saving. I had a fair chance, for my weekly wages were grossing up to £25 with a net packet of more than £20. That was good enough for big saving in my sort of world, and the firm paid £10 out of it every week into the trustee savings bank for me. Anything left over was my wife's housekeeping money, and after that I scrambled for pocket money.

Because life is what it is there were times when my system slipped a bit. I was coming away from the pay office one Friday when a melter I knew, named Baldwin, asked me to loan him five pounds. This was well outside the usual melting shop borrowing which generally amounted to a quick half dollar or so. I didn't want to give it and there were no reasons why I should give it. One reason for not loaning it stood out—Baldwin could never pay it back. Though he was only young, thirty-five or so, his health was shocking, and he rarely drew a full week's wages. There were periods when he was down for three and four months. He was indeed a bad risk so I decided to present him with two pounds, and thus salvage the other three. I looked at his anxious face as I started to tell him so, so I changed my mind and handed him the five pounds. He died six months afterwards and I reckoned it was the best money I ever spent, for value I mean.

In the summer of 1958 my daughter Bernadette quit her studies without achieving a diploma for design. That was disappointing for her mother and me; it disturbed our vanity. It didn't disturb Bernadette any, for she seemed perfectly happy with the tall young fellow who had interrupted her studies. I had a lot to say to her, mostly reproachful, and to him too, then suddenly in a rare flash of wisdom I realised that the lad and my girl would marry, and that they would make a go of it. So I shut up and am glad I did, for that's the way it happened.

Just to make sure, or so it seemed, that I should make steel until retiring time, the firm invested in a fettling machine. It was a clumsy looking affair but very mobile and tremendously effective and it banished for ever the old shovel and swing method of repairing furnace baths. It streamed the finely crushed dolomite from its bunker into the damaged parts with effortless ease, while we melters stood by and watched. With its arrival it seemed to me that the last vestiges of the oldtime steelmaking methods had disappeared, and a good riddance too. But what a wonderful thing if it had suddenly landed on the melting shop a quarter of a century previously, in the days before the basic brick furnace arrived to send the silica brick furnace packing. Then the silica dripping in over-heated furnaces tore the baths to pieces, and tore the melters to pieces in their efforts to rebuild them.

With the fettling machine's arrival there was but little manual labour left in my working day. I was free to concentrate upon the welfare of my furnace and its contents and that's the way it should be for good steelmaking. Across the way, just fifty yards or so, was a new steel plant built since the second world war, with 300 tons capacity open hearth tilting furnaces. They were in the forefront of modernity but not for long, for the pure oxygen method of steelmaking was on its way rapidly. We had new rolling mills laid down, and new blast furnaces, and the more millions the company spent the more pleased I was to be quitting it all soon. Pleased but not anxious about it, for it was interesting looking on at all the progress around me. But the greater the progress the more I felt an anachronism, I who had actually seen men make steel on cold metal, hand-charging furnaces. So when the time came I got out just like I hoped I would. The fellows must have thought something about me for they gave me the greatest presentation ever any man had on retiring from the melting shop.

22

Writing Man

Once I quit the melting shop it didn't take me long to get used to doing without it. Something good I felt had happened to the beginning and end of each day. There was no longer need to rise at half-past four in the mornings, and no longer the need to go out on nightshifts. That gave me the chance to put a little even tenor in my life and to try to do some of the things I had always wanted to do.

Everything was in my favour, my health had improved and there was no sickness in my home, and that made all the difference in the world.

I've heard men say in retirement that they were lonely most of all for the company of men. I've experienced loneliness too at times, but not specifically for the company of men. Rather I have enjoyed the loneliness, for I knew it would end at my own front door. If it ever comes that my wife is no longer there to greet me, then, and then only, will I know real loneliness.

The drastic cut in my income didn't bother me much; I was rather glad that I was poor, not poverty-stricken, just poor. It was an incentive to me to get my pounding finger on my portable typewriter and earn, earn, earn. Since as long as I remember my idea of heaven was a small cheque, and with 'the editor's compliments'. I had achieved it intermittently throughout the years from as far back as 1923, and before that I had first hit print without pay in 1912. I think I would have done better still in a less exhausting trade, for I started many, many articles and never finished them. Weariness I found was not conducive to good and sustained writing.

Yet not once in all the years had I let go the belief that I could write. I was certain of that whereas I was a doubtful, hesitant fellow in nearly everything else. For me there was no prouder title, nothing I wanted more than to be a writing man. I had no interest in writing novels and no hope that I could ever do so, and very little interest in short story writing. What I liked to write was articles of one or two or three thousand words. With less desire for deliberate study, and more for the sheer interest, I pursued every correspondence course the W.E.A. offered in literature and in English, they were all very good. I read many books on the technique of writing and many of them were helpful and interesting too.

Then when I quit work I joined the literary study group in the Manchester College of Adult Education. Save for my son-in-law, John Pennington, it was the first time I conversed with people who were really interested in writing. John makes his living writing for television and radio and he said to me one day, 'I'm submitting some work to the B.B.C. so you write a piece and I'll take it along with me.' So I wrote a piece about steelmaking in a heatwave and the B.B.C. bought it. I recorded it too and it went on the air during the fifteen minutes interlude of a symphony concert.

This was a big thing indeed for me, an astonishing thing, and I followed it up with two more recordings, shorter ones, and a lot of rejections. I contributed to magazines and during a long period only one bought anything I wrote. That didn't bother me much for by then I was in full swing, a lonely but far from unhappy figure battering away with one finger on a very old portable. After years of steelmaking it is impossible for me to touch type. I hit the keys hard so that I perforate too—in that way at least my words sink in.

From articles and radio I went to letter writing and if it was a descent then I didn't notice it. I was a writer for money and not without integrity I hoped, and a guinea for an interesting letter was something I did not despise. I did very well too and had an eight guineas cheque for my top figure. Talking about integrity, I noticed that each payment I received made me increasingly determined to give value for money. Small though my sphere, I liked the idea of being a responsible writer as well as the next man.

Just to vary things and because it was an adventure for me I sat my G.C.E. 'O' levels in English Literature and in English. My studies occupied the whole of a winter and a schoolmaster friend gave me much help. I managed a bare pass in English and just failed one in Literature. I lacked technique more than knowledge, I should have used every minute to the best advantage and I didn't. But no odds, I enjoyed it anyway and I had no future to worry over and no angry parents to assuage. The only person really concerned was my wife and she thought I was wonderful for entering at all.

When my typing fingers grew weary and my studies grew cold, I dropped everything and made for the wide open spaces, well nearly, I went to my allotment. It is the end plot and right against a quite busy road, that means I cultivate acquaintances as well as cabbages. The majority of people pass by without a glance, and some pause for a word or two and then away. But there are some who prop their elbows on the low wall and prepare for a long stay. It makes no odds that I don't know them, that I'm busy and wish to remain busy. They take no notice of that, they have something to say and the time to say it and nothing is going to stop them. Then I straighten up, for I always consider it bad manners to be bent down when people are talking to me, and I listen for as long as they care to stay.

The conversations are interesting at times, and even profitable. For once I wrote an article about them and sold it to a magazine at a good price. The cheque for it was almost as good as a week on the furnaces, and there was no sweating or going on nightshift for it. I felt somewhat bewildered about that, for I found it a bit hard to believe that money can be honestly earned without the sweat from one's brow. However, the cure for that may be repetition; if I keep holding my hand out more and more then the extraordinary may become the commonplace.

Still that's doubtful in my case; for me an editor's acceptance of anything I write will always be an event. It was never more so than when I reached the pages of *New Statesman*. That was the greatest thrill of my life and from then on I reckoned that I really was a writing man. The article was simple enough; it could be no other, for I am essentially a simple man. In it I explained how I tackled the problem of retirement and how there was no problem after I picked up my pen. I was well paid for it and my fee was augmented by an anonymous gentleman, or maybe a lady, who forwarded me ten pounds in appreciation.

That was splendid but there was more, I received letters of appreciation addressed me c/o *New Statesman* from America, Canada, Greece, Indonesia, Nairobi, Italy, as well as from people in England. Such a scope delighted me and I wondered how far round the earth the magazine did travel each week. There were also requests to write for radio and for other magazines and I was glad to oblige. I answered all letters and without duplication and to each one I gave a sample of my best work free. Since the letters didn't cease coming for four months and I kept on answering them, it seemed I had a job for life.

In the end of course it all finished, but the benefits remain, for I still write for radio and for magazines, and at the editor's request if you please. There's no vast living behind it, no fortune, but I'm doing the thing I love best. Often enough it gives me a cheque in the hand, and one in the bush, and by heaven that's fortune enough for me.

Sometimes I think of the furnaces, but only to tell myself that I'm glad that we've parted. I hold nothing against them; I escaped almost whole where they tore many a better man to ribbons, but I wouldn't care to do it all over again. The one thing steel gave me besides my wages was the satisfaction of creation. The firm provided the wherewithal but I made the steel and therein lay myself respect and my prestige. A steel melter was a somebody in the world of heavy industry. He still is and I hope he always will be.